*"What I found that day was so sim
mind. This is the missing link an
psychiatry were searching for. T
millions of people who were suffering needlessly."*

**Sydney Banks**, on his 1973 enlightenment experience and his vision for psychology and psychiatry—as read by **Dr. Keith Blevens** from his unpublished book—and viewed on the *Addiction, Alcoholism & The 3 Principles* "Golden Moments" video series. https://youtu.be/Ry6hc5tSsUU

\* \* \*

*"I can attest with certainty that '**Evolution of Addiction Recovery**' is pure truth. Harry Derbitsky, in his down-to-earth, no-holds-barred, heartfelt conviction in the innate mental well-being of all human beings, and in his pointing to the power of an insight-based understanding of the 3 universal Principles as the road home, has presented a genuine beacon of hope and health for those who, in their search for peace, have struggled with addiction in any form. I strongly encourage anyone who desires more love and peace in their life to read this unique book."*

**Dr. William Pettit Jr.,** MD, is a board-certified psychiatrist and co-owner of 3 Principles Intervention LLC. He has spent the majority of his career awakening mental health and the sharing of the understanding that there is just one cause—and one cure—for mental illness. Dr. Pettit is a recognized educator in the 3 Principles intervention, and he has presented at many national and international conferences, as well as consulted to numerous clients both nationally and internationally.

\* \* \*

i

*"As Harry says, when we move from trying to fix the 'problem' of addiction, to speaking to the spirit in those who are suffering, consciousness rises and incredible transformation often takes place. I have unequivocally seen this to be true with my own clients, and I know it is true for others who share these Principles that Harry points toward. 'Evolution of Addiction Recovery' points to what can be a complete paradigm shift in treating addiction, as well as in how we view mental health."*

**Dr. Amy Johnson**, PhD, is a psychologist, coach, author, and speaker who shares a 3 Principles approach that helps people find true, lasting freedom from unwanted habits via insight rather than willpower. She is author of several books including *The Little Book of Big Change: The No-Willpower Approach to Breaking Any Habit* (2016); and in 2017, she opened The Little School of Big Change. She has been a regularly featured expert on *The Steve Harvey Show* and Oprah.com, as well as in *The Wall Street Journal* and *Self* magazine.

*Psychology without Spirituality*

*is like a person dying from lack of water*

*in the middle of the Sahara Desert,*

*sitting down for a drink*

*with a tall, empty glass.*

*The glass looks hopeful,*

*but the person still dies.*

—Harold Derbitsky

# EVOLUTION OF ADDICTION RECOVERY

## BOOK 1

**Harold (Harry) Derbitsky**

# The Author's Perspective

The term MIND, as it appears in this book, is a psychological term for God. The 3 Principles, mentioned throughout this book, lead and point us to an experience of God. Sydney Banks uncovered these 3 Principles—MIND, THOUGHT and CONSCIOUSNESS—but he did not lay claim to them. Rather, MIND allowed the uncovering to happen through him. The fact that he shared these 3 Principles with the world, including me, simply means we are the lucky ones to be exposed to his teachings and enlightenment.

In the Indigenous world to which I have also been exposed and of which I have shared about in this book, Spirit is another name for MIND. The only authenticity one needs in life is for Spirit to let us know who we are and that it loves what we are doing. When we experience a lower level of life, it is also healthy for us—it cleans us out and lets us know life is spiritual. It is a signal.

What do I mean by that? I mean that every time I step into my addictive behaviour cycle—or, at least, what I believe to be my addictive cycle—MIND sends me a signal that I need to wake up. I am stuck in time, I am paying attention to the wrong stuff, and I need to wake up! MIND has a new direction for me, and all I have to do is get out of my head. It is so simple. I experience discomfort in the short term so that I can hear what is needed in the long term.

For example, when I began writing this book, I had one concept—the wrong concept! I was going to write about how to deliver a perfect program about addiction, and this program would be super successful. But, I was not ready for that book.

The book I did write is an expression of what I know at the present time. That is why I am calling it "Book 1." And it was time to write it now. Whereas, before, there was no inspiration, no energy to write, because I was not writing me. I was writing a belief. A belief is powerless, the truth is all powerful.

So, this book has been easy to produce because *I* have not written it. It has written itself and has taught me, and it has come effortlessly and easily. I hope it will help many, but even if it only helps a few, then I am happy.

Sydney Banks's teachings are interlaced throughout this book; because it is through them that I have recovered from a life of confusion and have become a happy and contented human being. His teachings, guidance, and modelling have inspired me to uncover more of who I am. My gratitude is immense!

The 3 Principles of MIND, THOUGHT and CONSCIOUSNESS as uncovered by Sydney Banks are a spiritual psychology. They are a breakthrough in the evolution of addiction recovery.

# The Author's Story

My story is not that easy to describe. I teach the 3 Principles in many areas, not only addiction recovery. Even in the recovery field, it may be confusing. While I have never been addicted to a substance, I have, of course, experienced addictive behavioural patterns, such as overeating, anger, and zealous ambition. All of these, I have found, are created from fear and insecurity. And from an even profounder understanding, the root of fear and insecurity is thought.

Thus, whether I am teaching mental well-being, True Self, the power of a secure mind, or addictive recovery, the messages are similar in that the 3 Principles understanding is the origin of all feelings and experiences.

I have surprised myself by giving live talks in Europe and North America and global webinars including participants in Europe, and North and South America. I am delighted to share what I know with so many beautiful and wise people throughout the world. I am also delighted that some seem to like my message of the mystical nature of the Principles, along with having a good time and sharing laughter.

I have had several major breakthroughs in my life, which I have attempted to share in this book, along with other contributory insights. The first major breakthrough was in 1976 when I lived on Salt Spring Island along with others known as "the Salt Spring-ers," who listened to and learned pearls of wisdom from Sydney Banks. It was there that I had my defining insight—that life is spiritual! And that I was part of this spiritual reality we call "life." I then had to wait until 2016 before quietly walking into another reality. I call it the "world of contentment." It was in this heightened awareness that I received a phone call that was to change my outward life.

The night before this call, I had had a prayer to—or talk with—God, that went something like this: "Well, God, I am not bored, and I am very satisfied, but it seems like I could use a little more stimulation in my life wherein I share some of what I have come to love." I then went to sleep, and the moment I woke up, the phone rang. A chap whom I had taught many years before said that he had been offered another job, and he wondered if I would like to take over a teaching position for a small program at a recovery centre in downtown Vancouver. My immediate impulse was to say something like, "Oh, I hate teaching about addiction. That is my worst area, and the one in which I have always been the least successful."

But I had just prayed, so I said, "I would give it a try." To my surprise, when I soon went in the centre and talked with people there, it was different than ever before.

I would like readers to understand this difference. Previously, when addressing clients, I had been trying to fix the problem of addiction. This time around, I was no longer talking about the problem at all. Without any conscious effort, my understanding had quietly changed. My clients, I now saw, were innately healthy, and so I just talked to the spirit within, as I like to describe it.

To my surprise, the clients loved it. They, of course, already knew a tremendous amount about the spiritual nature of life. They listened deeply because they really wanted to learn something new, not the same old stuff. I loved that, because in other areas of teachings, clients often did not really want to change. These clients appreciated the honesty and genuineness of my offerings. And we had a lot of fun. Laughter was prevalent along with powerful feelings of hope. Yes, I loved it!

Other programs followed for those in recovery and also for the homeless. This led to the initiation of the twice-a-month webinar series for the "Addictions, Alcoholism & The 3 Principles" Facebook group, along with my brilliant co-host, Greg Suchy, of Akron, Ohio. Participants from all over the world have attended and participated in the webinars, and to our surprise, the after views of the recordings became one of the major areas of success. And many went on to view the other recordings in the series on our YouTube channel, *Addictions, Alcoholism & The 3 Principles.*

This led me into a new phase, sharing with people internationally on the topic of addiction. Before that, I had primarily centered my sharing among the Indigenous People of North America. I had stepped inside the bubble of the Indigenous world, but I had found it extremely difficult to share any of my experiences with others outside the bubble, including the 3 Principles community. Entering the realm of addiction recovery, however, brought about a different result; it seemed almost everyone was interested in addiction recovery as it is obviously one of the largest social and human problems facing our world today.

So, at age 69, my life expanded and continues to become more interesting, more stimulating and more rewarding than ever before. Go figure. Everyone says that at my age we need to retire and slow down, but the opposite happened to me. My life is so rewarding that I often think I have gone to heaven. Yet, it is so ordinary, because all I am doing is being Harry.

In truth, that is all I know. As long as I am Harry, life will be good and rewarding. Maybe it will not always be a smooth ride, but it will always be the thrill of the moment and the joy of living my life contentedly.

All my Relations, (Indigenous meaning: "We are all related, All are related.")

Harold (Harry) Derbitsky, *Harry (Standing Elk)*

# Points of Reference

1. Throughout the book, whenever any of the 3 Principles—Mind, Thought and Consciousness—are being discussed, they will be expressed in the small-capitals font in order indicate that an actual Principle is what is being referred to. Usage of "mind," "thought" and "consciousness" in any other font, then, refers to personal thoughts, minds or consciousness.

2. The "Addiction, Alcoholism & The 3 Principles" webinar series:
   - facilitated by Greg Suchy, Recovery Coach (Akron, Ohio, USA) and Harold Derbitsky of ACT Training Inc. (Vancouver, B.C., Canada)
   - All episodes can be found on the YouTube channel *Addiction, Alcoholism & The 3 Principles*. <https://www.youtube.com/channel/UC6y_NNYUW6YHqFILz7 iSmjQ/videos>

   Also on the channel, you will find another section called the "Golden Moments Course," which I highly recommend as a starting point.

3. When this author talks about "going inside or within," or "going inside ourselves," he does not mean we should go within or deep down into our bodies. It is a *metaphor* indicating the spiritual reality that lies within every human being. It could just as easily be called soul, innate health, spirit or our own consciousness. It is formless,

and thus not an aspect of the body, which is obviously, already formed.

4. Sydney Banks's books and videos are available for purchase from Amazon and Lone Pine Publishing. All books or videos illustrated in this book are by Sydney Banks.
   a. A *free* website where the readers can find several of Sydney Banks's full-length streaming videos, as well as book excerpts and audio clips from talks: www.sydbanks.com
   b. Another free and recommended website with Sydney Banks's later words, books, stories, reflections, and videos: www.sydneybanks.org
   c. The Three Principles School was founded in 2008, by Chip Chipman and Elsie Spittle, at the request of Sydney Banks: www.threeprinciplesfoundation.org

5. My gratitude for the editing of the book goes to Certified Transformative Coach and professional book editor, Joel Drazner (drazedit@mac.com).

6. Harold Derbitsky is President of ACT (Advanced Coaches Training) Training Inc. Visit the ACT website—www.acttraining.biz—for all necessary contact information.

# Table of Contents

# Preface: Einstein on Thought

I remember seeing a documentary film on Albert Einstein that explored his way of seeing life. One of his gifts was his mystical ability to visualize "thought experiments" in order to explain what only he could see. Arising from the mind of one man, these visual images served as thought-related models that allowed him to understand on a larger scale the entire physical universe.

Einstein demonstrated mathematically how time and space are shaped by matter, and not vice versa. In a thought experiment he devised, he asks us to imagine that both the front and rear of a speeding train are struck by lightning bolts. To an observer standing on an embankment watching this hypothetical train, the two lightning bolts strike the train simultaneously. An observer sitting midpoint on the train, however, would experience a slight time gap between the bolt that hits the front part and the bolt that hits the rear. Einstein's curiosity about this phenomenon ultimately led him to the conclusion that gravity and acceleration not only felt the same but are the same. His evolution produced such genius discoveries as the General Theory of Relativity and $E=MC^2$. He visualized a higher and more-correct way of seeing life, gravity and the laws of nature, a perspective quite different from the way most of humankind had perceived them.

Here is my thought-experiment question: *Does addiction create the thoughts or does THOUGHT create the addiction?* This is a fundamental question, because if addiction creates our thoughts, then present-day status quo approaches are fine. If, however, THOUGHT creates the addiction, then psychological and 12-Step approaches must include this truth as part of their philosophy or teachings. Einstein hated conflict in theories. So do I, and much of this book is aimed at answering this question.

# Introduction

As one who teaches the Principles of MIND, THOUGHT and CONSCIOUSNESS—as uncovered by Sydney Banks—to people who are addicted as well as to the non-addicted, it has become obvious to me that the opioid crisis and alcoholism have become the world's top social problems. The 12-Step programs, psychotherapy and Christian-based recovery systems produce inconsistent results, and they sometimes also innocently misdirect the minds of the addicted. So, not only are the answers society has offered not working for many, but also the number of people addicted—regardless of race, color or economic foundation—is growing at an alarming pace. This unfortunate trend is fueled by growing trauma, chronic stress and the general lowering of mental health experienced by many in our general population. More and more people are looking to opiates, alcohol, pharmaceuticals or street drugs to relieve their social anxiety, confusion and the low moods they are experiencing. Thus, they become trapped in a negative spiral of thinking these drugs are the best relief for their minds, with disastrous side effects (i.e., addiction, homelessness and death). Almost 400,000 people died in the USA from opioid overdoses between 1999 and 2017, according to the Centers for Disease Control and Prevention (CDC). There is also a host of serious secondary social conflicts and criminal activities linked to the illegal production and distribution of drugs.

In this book, *opiates* refers to drugs that are naturally derived from the poppy (*Papaver somniferum*), and there are both pharmaceutical and street-drug varieties. Opium and morphine have long been two of the most commonly misused opiates, whether recreationally or as pain relievers. *Opioids*, on the other hand, are synthetic opiates, which are related to naturally derived opiates because of their structure and how they produce opiate-like effects. Heroin is a semi-synthetic opiate, and it is considered one of the most dangerous recreational drugs in the world. Some examples of synthetic opioids include the prescription painkillers hydrocodone (Vicodin) and oxycodone (OxyContin), as well as fentanyl and methadone. There is a rapidly growing global crisis of addiction to both opiates and opioids.

Opioids, such as heroin or prescription medications, are considered sedatives and their effects include drowsiness, slowed breathing and euphoria. Not all drug users seek these effects, some look for a burst of energy. Methamphetamine (meth) and cocaine (crack cocaine is the crystal and most powerful form of this drug) are considered "uppers," resulting in increased heart rate and breathing rate, increased blood pressure and increased energy. While North America has been focused on the abuse of opioids, the use of uppers, such as methamphetamine, and "party drugs" such as ecstasy and Molly, has been increasing behind the scenes.

The topic of addiction must, of course, include alcohol, and this book also addresses the destructive nature of alcohol abuse within the Indigenous populations of North America. Alcohol is a central nervous system depressant, which means that consuming alcohol reduces, or inhibits, overall brain activity. Those whose brains have adapted to frequent drinking by increasing glutamate signaling will then experience withdrawal symptoms like tremors, hallucinations, and convulsions if they stop drinking. This occurs because their brain will be too stimulated. Once drinkers have reached this point, normal human functioning often ceases and they become overwhelmed.

I am not suggesting that 12-Step programs do not have their successes, because to date they have obviously helped more humans who are addicted than any other approach. But by now, it should be obvious that the opioid crisis and alcoholism cannot be ignored or left to non-evolving approaches. I am simply pointing the reader and clients to what I see as the truth in addiction recovery, and directing them to their own inner wisdom, where all answers lay waiting. These 3 Principles will evolve humankind to a brand-new way of thinking, and isn't that our dream for addiction?

"EVEN GOOD PRINCIPLES CAN SOMETIMES BE DISPLACED BY THE DISCOVERY OF STILL BETTER ONES. ONLY GOD IS UNCHANGING."

*Bill Wilson*

"Bill Wilson was a proponent of the evolution of recovery. He believed that we should never get stuck on something that's working when something better comes along. This does not mean the old way is wrong or bad any more than saying vegetables are healthier than fruit, which may infer that fruit is unhealthy."

—*Greg Suchy, recovery coach and co-host of the "Addiction, Alcoholism & The 3 Principles" webinar series*

## TWO CONCEPTS IN THIS BOOK

### 1. THE TRUTH WILL SET YOU FREE

### 2. SEEING WHAT IS FALSE WILL SET YOU FREE

"There are estimates of 1-2 million people sober worldwide via A.A. What Sydney Banks saw seems to be the next evolution. Bill Wilson, in creating the 12 steps, was doing the best he could to describe what happened to him (while borrowing from the Oxford movement).

And, in fairness, virtually everyone I have come across in A.A. is having a much better life with a spiritual core than they were previously. However, the 'missing link,' which Sydney Banks pointed to so clearly is that, at our essence, we were never broken. And that the *entirety of our distress* is always coming from THOUGHT in the moment. This last bit is certainly not fully grasped in many A.A. meetings, though there are hints in the literature.

If Sydney Banks's work really took hold in the 12-Step world, as well as for those still experiencing addiction, the spread could be huge."

*—Christian McNeill (elementsofwellbeing.net) is a 3 Principles Transformational Coach and hosts the Three Principles Conversations series. She is a former lawyer, living in Glasgow, Scotland. At the start of 2011, she came across the 3 Principles, which touched her life as deeply as had her becoming sober in 1988.*

* * *

## WHO IS THE AUDIENCE FOR THIS BOOK?

The audience for this book is anyone wanting to gather a fuller understanding of addiction. This includes the lady at the recovery center who asked me, "Why doesn't the 12-Step program work?"; and those who are openly loyal to the 12-Step program because they feel it has saved their lives. It also may be for those who look for answers via psychotherapy or religion, those who have simply given up, or those who are the support mechanism for those beautiful souls who have become addicted. This book may provide mentorship to those offering professional services in the field of addiction, and it may offer clarity to 3P practitioners.

SECTION 1

**UNIQUE MERITS OF THE 3 PRINCIPLES**

**IN THE FIELD OF ADDICTION AND ALCOHOLISM**

# Chapter 1

## Is Teaching the 3 Principles, as Uncovered by Sydney Banks, Effective in Treating Addiction, Alcoholism and Human Suffering?

The answer is a resounding YES! And if you are lucky enough to find this book intriguing, you may find that you have uncovered the greatest secret in the world, and the most valuable.

The 3 Principles of MIND, THOUGHT and CONSCIOUSNESS—which will be explained throughout, and specifically later in this book—are a spiritual psychology. They explain the workings of the human experience *in totality*—this includes all happiness, all suffering, and all mental-health issues.

Even more important, since you yourself are these 3 Principles, by coming to understand or insightfully see them, they will reveal to you your spiritual or True Self.

For much of his life, Einstein pursued a "unified field theory," while Stephen Hawking's dream was to uncover the "Theory of Everything." The way I see it, the unified theory of life they searched for has been uncovered by Sydney Banks. As he declared in his book *The Enlightened Gardener Revisited*:

### MIND + CONSCIOUSNESS +THOUGHT = Reality

Mr. Banks always emphasized that when he was talking about "mind," he meant the universal or divine MIND, not the personal mind; the same for CONSCIOUSNESS and THOUGHT.

What this author sees is that virtually all the historic religions, at their essence, are always pointing to a spiritual awakening that originates in the formless energy. MIND, THOUGHT and CONSCIOUSNESS are the spiritual tools of the formless energy of everything. God needs tools just like a gardener does.

If readers will have a little patience and an open mind to the possibility that the above is true, they, too, may uncover the usefulness of these spiritual Principles.

# Chapter 2

## The Psychological Reality We Live In

I had already experienced the Oneness of life while living on Salt Spring Island off the coast of Vancouver, Canada. My Oneness experience occurred while in pure silence for three or four minutes. It felt like an eternity in which I was fully aware of everything including the understanding that I and all life are Spirit! I will describe this experience in more detail later in this book.

In my second powerful experience, I discovered the missing link required for living a happy, contented life here on earth. This led to my liberation from being a victim of my cravings, urges, and moods; from my blaming the "treachery of the world" and my bad luck; and from much of my immaturity and many of my bad habits.

Dr. Keith Blevens, a 3P practitioner and psychologist (threeprinciplesparadigm.com), possesses a strong understanding of the simple logic of how a *thought creates a feeling*. On one of his instructional videos, titled "It Only Works One Way," he asks which of the following is true:

1. Feelings are coming from what is happening to us.

OR

2. Feelings are coming from our thinking about what is happening to us.

He follows with, "One is true, and one is not true—can you see which one?"

Later in the video, he mentions that he was in a lower mood the previous evening when his wife asked him:

1. Are your feelings coming from your thinking?

OR

2. Are they coming from what you are thinking about?

Insightfully, he recognizes that his feelings are not coming from the content but from the thinking about the content. This freed him totally! Dr. Blevens suggests that when we understand where our thoughts are coming from or where they are *not* coming from, it quiets one's mind and truth is seen. This is an aspect of how the logic of the human experience works.

Dr. Blevens shows us one example of how the psychological community is teaching the 3 Principles. Since I am not a psychologist, I had to experience the concept that "THOUGHT creates feeling" in a totally different manner, and the expression and my experience of it demonstrates this. When I invited Dr. Blevens to our "Addiction, Alcoholism & The 3 Principles" webinar series, his way of explaining helped me to more fully understand the expansive nature of my own insight.


## MY DAY WITH SYDNEY BANKS MANY YEARS AGO

It was a picturesque, sunny day in the early 1990s as I drove my Nissan ZX Turbo 300 sports car, with its T-top roof removed, off the ferry on the way to Sydney Banks's home. Syd lived in a Salt Spring Island home with a panoramic view of the ocean and Trincomali Heights. When his smiling face greeted me, I felt elated.

We both were in a fun-loving mood, and Syd suggested we take a drive for some lunch. We spent over an hour eating at Dagwood's restaurant, a popular local eatery that is famous for its plain setting and delicious, huge portions. Then we drove around Salt Spring with Fergus, Syd's sheepdog, who sat in the back seat with his head out of the roof, as if the car was his chariot and he was the King of the World. Syd was delighted because Fergus was happy—simply put, he loved Fergus.

I enjoyed hanging out with Syd, especially when we were just pals. But, of course, I had not taken the three-hour ferry ride just to hang out—I had come for a deeper understanding of life.

It was a rare moment in my life. I had just been hired as the executive director of the Aboriginal Foster Children's Association in Vancouver. This was a position I would hold for only a few months, but at that time, it represented a great opportunity to share what I understood with the Indigenous community.

Syd suggested that we drive back toward the ferry, where there is an isolated walk up to the edge of cliffs overlooking the side of the ocean and where the ferry comes from Vancouver to Salt Spring Island. I parked, and off the three of us went up the walk. It only took about ten minutes to climb to the viewpoint; Fergus, Syd and Harry—three pals loving every moment of the sacred feelings being expressed by the beauty of nature.

When we arrived at the top, I stood at the edge of the cliff overlooking the ocean and neighboring islands. Suddenly, Syd said, "OK, shoot. Ask me any question you want."

Let me explain the unusualness of that moment from my perspective. Here I was, standing on the edge of a cliff overlooking heaven with an enlightened man with the highest level of consciousness that I have ever been exposed to, a man who understood the meaning of life and our connection to God, and he was inviting me to ask any question I wanted. Surprisingly, I was not intimidated. In fact, I was enjoying myself, and I proceeded to ask him about 10 spiritual questions.

He answered every question calmly and ended every explanation with the same statement, "It's all One." This was interesting, I thought, because whenever someone asked me a question, I would just answer the question. Syd, however, always added, "It's all One."

Then I asked him another question, one that I cannot remember, and ALL OF A SUDDEN, IT HAPPENED!!

As I was asking the question, I saw, as clearly as anything I have ever seen (much like a lightning bolt), *a thought jump out of my mouth and BOOMERANG right back into my body as a feeling.* This boomerang totally caught my attention, releasing another question, "Who was the thinker?!" And with this inquiry, I could see that I was the one who was causing all my suffering with my thinking.

Until that time, I'd had the impression that the process went like this: I thought and then later in my life or many lives later, I would face the consequences of my negative thinking, which certain Hindu and Buddhist schools describe as the workings of karma. However, this was more like "instant karma." I now was aware that my thoughts created an instant feeling. Thought and feeling are not separated. They are One.

This "boomerang effect" had brought with it a heightened level of understanding that not only freed me from much of my suffering but allowed me to see a whole new world. It was as though this new understanding uncovered something in me that had been blocked off by my antiquated beliefs.

Syd and I talked about the boomerang and other things, but this was the beginning of my realization of how powerful THOUGHT is, and how freeing this understanding can be for all humans. I have continued to experience deeper and deeper insights into this "boomerang effect," which has resolved many of my misunderstandings about the origin of THOUGHT. The boomerang was the icebreaker that allowed me to walk with much more psychological freedom in this world. Syd facilitated and was the catalyst for this spiritual-psychological insight, yet the experience had nothing to do with him. The space we experienced together had freed my consciousness to explore the horizons of the universe.

This powerful experience was the first time I had an insight regarding the psychological aspect of the 3 Principles. When I lived on Salt Spring from 1976 to 1981, I and many of the old-time Salt Spring Islanders were basically attracted to Sydney Banks's predominant message of spiritual truth. When he had shifted directions, so to speak, as many psychologists like Dr. Roger Mills, Dr. George Pransky, and the above-mentioned Dr. Keith Blevens, to name a few, were being attracted to the power of truth that he had uncovered, I found that I had no interest in this spiritual-psychological direction. After the boomerang experience, I saw, increasingly, that I had been too narrow in my beliefs. Once again, I had to say, "Thank you, Sydney Banks." I can see him on the "other side" smiling!


"And here lies the secret to mental health,
when you can find the connection between thought and what you call reality." — Sydney Banks

# Chapter 3

# The Victim Story

During a discussion as part of a YouTube series Christian Olsen and I co-hosted in 2017-18 (under the title *Hope & Challenges - Three Principles in Action in Denmark*), Christian brought up the very interesting concept that the continuation of addiction results from addicts' belief in their own victim story. This victim story hypothesis can appear to be true, so let's take a look at the idea in relation to the previous chapter.

If people feel they are victims of circumstances or bad luck, then they innocently believe that outside circumstances control their thoughts. While the world of present-day psychology often professes this to be true, and many people believe that this is true, that does not make it true!

Barbara Sarah Smith, MSW, who is a 3P-based addictions psychotherapist, told me she is so glad her clients do not think that their thinking is created or controlled by outside circumstances. This simple realization helps them to wake up. It tackles the psychological belief that we are a product of our past, and that we cannot change this. I am not talking about change using our willpower; I am talking about change using a higher level of understanding.

This concept is much like an example Dr. Keith Blevens gives in his video series mentioned in the previous chapter: In bygone days, people believed that the world was flat. This belief directly affected how ships were navigated. The ships stayed close to land and also had a huge anchor on board. Sailors feared that if they travelled too far, they would simply reach the edge of the world and fall off. When it was discovered that the world was round, all the old ways of navigating changed, and the business of selling large anchors also greatly diminished.

Now, let us bring in the boomerang effect of thought and feelings. If one experiences a negative feeling, the cause is a negative thought. Negative feelings, which are based on fear and insecurity, often compound into a stressful moment-to-moment reality. It would be difficult to argue that stress is not a factor in the addictive thought patterns of life. Obviously, the removal of stress, and instead being happy and content, leads one to a higher level of mental health and much greater enjoyment of this strange animal we call "our life." The recognition of the relationship between thought and our life can be as life changing as was the revelation that the world is round instead of flat.

We are not victims of our feelings, and we do not have to think 100 times each day about how we *are* victims. This negative thinking pattern perpetuates the feelings of victimization. It is a false god or "a false image of self-importance," an expression Sydney Banks used to define *ego* in the early days. Believing oneself a victim is similar to believing the world is flat. While it is supported by many in our world, it is simply a belief that will change as truth is uncovered.

Vice versa, if we capture a beautiful feeling, we feel joy and beauty as we access wisdom and/or our spiritual identity. In the end, the simple answer is to change thought, thus changing the feeling in the moment, and this is the answer to being a victim or a loser. Once again, the 3 Principles unravel the mystery, this time the mystery of victimization.

I want to emphasize here what I often say:

> *The answer to all life and its problems lies in simplicity.*
> *If it is complicated, chances are it is coming from the intellect;*
> *it should be ignored.*

Sydney Banks could often be heard saying, "The simpler the better." It has taken me a lifetime to realize how profound these words are.

# Chapter 4

## Do Past Traumas Need To Be Re-Experienced and Purged Before Healing Can Take Place?

Downtown Vancouver, around the intersection of Main and Hastings, is the heart of the opiate and addiction crisis in this West Coast Canadian city, and it is the habitat for many people who are heavily addicted and homeless. Walking to a recovery centre where I used to teach, I would see hundreds of homeless people lying on the sidewalks, many of whom were shooting up or hanging out in dreadful alleys that smelled putrid and looked more like a place for rodents than human beings.

The recovery centre provides a detox floor (12 beds), where stays generally range from a few weeks to three months; and a transitional-housing floor (18 beds) where ongoing interim housing and recovery support is provided to residents post-detox.

The 3 Principles program I headed was open to all clients, and their participation was voluntary rather than mandatory. After the class, I was privileged to hand out Sydney Banks books that were generously donated to the program, but only if a client wished to have one. Never were books forced upon clients, nor was the intention to push my opinions on them.

Once, a lady of around 60, attending her initial class, decided she would like a book, so I handed her a copy of *The Enlightened Gardener*. This book is about an American psychologist who returns to England to talk again to the title character, a seemingly ordinary gardener. He and three other psychologists try to grasp the knowledge this gardener possesses regarding how the spiritual psychology of the 3 Principles will alleviate all human suffering.

In the following class, I noticed there was a bookmark in the book indicating she'd read almost half of it, so I asked her for her observations. People who are addicted are among the most honest people I see in society, one reason I love working with this segment. They know nonsense when they see or hear it, for they have been exposed to tons of it through their interactions in the system of psychologists, counselors, programs, administration, and religion. Not only was this client cuttingly honest in what she told me, but her observations led to a stimulating class discussion.

While she wasn't sure whether the ideas expressed in the book would help with addiction or in dealing with trauma, she could see how it might help some, but not all. And she said that everyone had to find out what was best for themselves, as other approaches might be more beneficial for some.

She also added, "What Sydney Banks, via *The Enlightened Gardener*, was suggesting was dramatically opposed to what the psychotherapists she was exposed to in her treatments were asserting. They were saying she must re-experience her past experiences of trauma, and only when this past sore was fixed, could she begin her healing process. Sydney Banks, on the other hand, through the words of the enlightened gardener, was saying that this is a misguided direction for healing. Going into the past to fix trauma and past problems would actually encourage the problems to become bigger and more powerful, to the pleasure of our analytical and intellectual minds or ego. His advice instead was to 'go inside,' and there we will uncover the wisdom we seek. He points to an insight being the spark of healing rather than willpower or the gathering of further information."

While I hoped the lady would read further into the book and garner a fuller understanding of the 3 Principles, she had already seen something significant and had touched on a controversial point in treating addiction.

Does one have to deal with past problems when they are suffering, or is it better to directly go to an "inside" spiritual feeling for the answers we all seek? And if we insightfully see the origin of THOUGHT rather than what our thoughts and the contents of them create, is that helpful to being free of addiction?

"Let your mind be still,

for the wisdom you seek is like that butterfly over yonder.

If you try to catch it with your intellect,

it will simply fly away.

On the other hand, if you can still your mind,

someday when you least expect it,

it will fall in the palm of your hand."

The evening of that class, over a delightful dinner with an Indigenous (Native) Elder, I brought up the topic of trauma. He explained that the Indigenous spiritual approach was to deal with the trauma first in a ceremony such as a sweat lodge, because the pain has been stored in the human for a long time and must be removed. I mentioned that you would not want to leave the person with that feeling, and he said, "No, we would not, and that is where Spirit comes in, and it frees them of their trauma; they are uplifted by Great Spirit into a higher experience of Spirit."

I casually told him I respected what he was describing, although it initially clashed with what I understood. I can see (and have seen) how that would work as long as the person is lifted out of that lower level of consciousness and out of the trauma or pain. What the ancient wisdom of Native spirituality seems to suggest is that when sufferers have totally exposed themselves to their past suffering, then the spiritual ceremonies elevate them to become One with the Spirit. Similarly, in 3P language, it allows them to experience a higher level of consciousness.

In psychotherapy, most often when a person is diagnosed with a traumatic mental health issue, the person is actually labeled with a chronic stress-related illness such as schizophrenia or bipolar disorder. Then medicine and counseling are applied to try to fix the person's problems. In the Indigenous world, the trauma is released, and the human being is guided home to their spiritual identity, thus receiving the healing specific to what they need.

When I mentioned the Indigenous way to healing to Sydney Banks, his first reaction was that going into the past was not good; in fact, he said, it was deadly. But when he heard it was part of their religion, he immediately changed his mind, stating that their religion must be respected, as that is their way.

Essentially, we have four different viewpoints:

    a) A psychotherapist labels someone as sick and tries to help that person to cope with the disease, usually condemning the person to a life of drugs and low self-esteem. Analyzing the past and talking about negative feelings are thought to be helpful and necessary.

    b) The 12-Step programs state emphatically that once addicted, we are diseased for the entirety of our lives.

    c) An Indigenous healer or shaman allows the human being to fully express their suffering and what is on their troubled mind; then Spirit and ceremony lifts the human being into a union with Great Spirit. They see Spirit and ceremony as being one and the same.

d) Sydney Banks, an enlightened man who uncovered the 3 Principles—the three spiritual principles of psychology—states that we all have the answers within, and that we always have a second chance, no matter our outside circumstances or past experiences. Going into the past to analyze our problems is quicksand.

"All you have to do is realize

that the past is now only a ghostly memory

kept alive by digging

into the archives of your own stagnated memories."


## My Conclusion

The form or problem cannot heal or be solved until we uncover the spiritual feelings within. The world of form is already defined while the healing power is expressed in the world of formlessness. I know this sounds ambiguous, yet, to my understanding, it is pure common sense.

By going to the source, that from which all was created, we do not have to always talk about our problems, we do not have to cure each problem individually, and, more important, we do not have to think about our problems, or, at least, not think about them over and over again. We want to flow with life. Some might call this denial, but it is not. When my level of consciousness rises, I forget my troubles, not because I am trying to. NO! It is because the nicer feelings take me into a nicer feeling about my life and about life in general. This is the freedom I aspire to and love. Then, when I look at my past struggles, they are most often seen as interesting and humorous evolvements of who I have become.

In the world of form—the world of our personal thinking—we create more form by thinking about things. This overactive thinking creates more and more form around the problem! The power of an insight is that it transforms "I am an addict" into seeing (as the 20th-century Jesuit philosopher Pierre Teilhard de Chardin first expressed) that we are "spiritual beings having a human experience," moment to moment. This ultimate answer is not a pretense; rather, it is a fact. Denial is simply the act of *not* going to the answer. Being in the Now is like coming home.

On a different day, in another class, a very interesting client talked about his life. He had been a very rich and successful contractor, building the most expensive houses in Vancouver. His business enabled him to own a yacht and a large mansion. He had a wife and kids and seemed to have everything that our world worships. Yet, for the prior two years, he had lived homeless on the streets, strung out much of the time on heroin. When asked about it by another classmate, he said that he had thought he could control it until he couldn't. But in that recovery class, he looked very confident and successful.

As we discussed what MIND is, he asked several questions until I suggested that there was something he didn't yet know. He knew a lot, and it was obvious to me that if he ever escaped his beliefs about addiction, he would be super successful in life once again. First, however, he had to realize that there was something he did not understand, and it was his puzzle to solve, not mine.

As we were talking, a feeling of hope stepped into his being. His face changed, his mood lightened, and he became optimistic about his chances of uncovering the answer to his puzzle. Somehow, an understanding of what MIND is, and of how THOUGHT creates a feeling, connected with him. There was a reason to this mess he had considered impossible to solve. As a result of attending the class and because of our discussion about MIND and insight, he had begun his journey to being connected with his True Self.

At the end of the class, I gave him a copy of *The Enlightened Gardener* and told him that the truth—the answer he is looking for—was in this book. I guaranteed it.

# Chapter 5

# The Spiritual and Psychological Worlds Are ONE

This is a biggie! One that the reader cannot see with the intellect but can only experience via the intuitive nature of MIND.

In our spiritual pursuits of understanding life and beyond, our little minds have no choice but to divide the worlds of spirit and form—we call this duality. We understand intuitively that the world of spirit and the world of material form do not operate under the same laws. (Or, do they?)

## Definition of the Two Worlds

The world of spirit is the invisible world of formlessness, which has no beginning or end. It exists before and after form, and inside you and me. In mathematical terms, *infinity* is the closest definition of spirit or God. In psychological terms, we use the word *mind* to describe God; and in this book, the spiritual principle of MIND means Big Mind, Spiritual Mind or Universal Mind. The reader can also use Christ Mind, Buddha Mind, Allah, Creator or any of the many other names in use. The world of spirit is not the world of religion, although religion has attempted to philosophically express this world to its greatest detail (sometimes correctly and other times, incorrectly).

The world of psychology is the expression of the form via THOUGHT, of that which originates from formlessness. It is all that we see, feel and experience through our personal lens or perspectives on life. We all have a personal mind. We all live in separate realities because we are all given the greatest gift in the world—free will to think whatever we want. And as Sydney Banks would say, "That is the problem."

Ego is an illusory reality we create through our own innocence, dishonesty and confusion. As previously mentioned, in the early days of his teachings, Sydney Banks would define *ego* as "an image of self-importance*"* and simplify it through the use of metaphoric expressions like "poor me" or "dig me." In my opinion, ego is the loud chatter and noise rattling around between our ears. This concept maker creates an illusion of life, and can you imagine how powerful this illusion becomes when, like bees to honey, it attracts thoughts from the negative past? Merciless! These concepts from the past are called *beliefs*; that which we hold as true but are not!

From Harry Derbitsky: *The Truth will set you free.*

*Beliefs will hold you prisoner.*

From Sydney Banks:

"All humans have the inner ability

to synchronize their *personal mind*

with the *impersonal mind* to

bring harmony into their lives."

**Personal Realization**

For much of my life, I walked with a misunderstanding of the above quote from *The Missing Link*. Because I believed in two different minds, I had to live in that understanding! I was unaware that I had actually been teaching the Oneness of life but with some false assumptions.

After Sydney Banks died in 2009, I became motivated to share more of what I had learned originally on Salt Spring Island. I was awakened, and life brought opportunities within the 3 Principles community. As I continued to pursue the elusive target of truth, I went to several conferences at the Three Principles School on Salt Spring in order to enrich my understanding and to become a better teacher of the Principles.

The school captured what Sydney was pointing to—the wise spiritual feelings inside every human being—but Elsie Spittle and Chip Chipman, the school's co-founders also understood how to include Sydney Banks and his teachings with their own teachings. Those attending often arrived at insights through experiencing the collective consciousness and the feeling of Sydney's spirit (wisdom) being in the room.

Each conference cracked certain misunderstandings of mine. At the last one I attended, though, I felt especially secure. The first day at that conference was very calming, filled with spiritual feelings.

For this conference, I had scored a lucky break. My dear friend had given me his comfortable home to stay in while he was busy off island. I had brought delicious food, much of which was already cooked, and I proceeded to relax and let my personal mind wander wherever it wanted to go within this idyllic setting. I took a pleasant walk. These are especially delightful on Salt Spring.

After one day of the conference, I was sitting in the evening with a cup of coffee, letting my cozy mind wander, when suddenly another bolt of lightning hit me. Earlier, Elsie had talked about her first personal insight being that "THOUGHT creates feeling." My knee-jerk reaction was, "That does not make sense. Elsie is so spiritual in her persona and wisdom, and yet, her insight is purely psychological."

I let this thought percolate and, genuinely curious, I decided I would raise it as a question in the next morning session. As luck would have it, Chip and Elsie did not start out with questions. After some general sharing of insights, Elsie then gave a spontaneous talk during which she stated as a matter of fact, "All insights are spiritual." This hit me hard. Immediately, I experienced a physical, mental and spiritual presence as though a mystical snake was slithering in an **S** formation from the top of my head to my bellybutton, moving and gyrating around my body. At the same time, it was as if seven or eight layers of skin were being removed, one layer at a time, leaving me exposed and raw. As the snake completed its rounds, connecting my left side in harmony with my right side, a mystical healing journey had been completed, and I realized that there is no difference between the psychological and spiritual—*they are One and the same.*

Before this insight, if I was teaching the spiritual, I was engaging in spiritual talk (the good stuff), and if I was teaching the psychological, I used different jargon and concepts and a different approach. But this dichotomy would never happen again. My own prejudice against psychology was over. I could now talk without judgment or concepts of good and bad. I could allow others to share without imposing my own interpretation, and best of all, I was free to be myself—a freedom I love with the greatest passion.

After the session, I mentioned this to Elsie, and she said, "Oh, what I talked about was very spiritual," and I mentioned how lucky it was that I could experience this for myself rather than having her telling me such.

Interestingly, after this insight, my respect for Elsie's wisdom magnified, but my reliance on her lessened. I saw her as a helper on my path of wisdom, with Sydney Banks being the One Who Knows.

### So, What Does Duality Have to Do With Addiction?

Everything! One answer to the cause of addiction lies in understanding duality. We can become addicted to foreign substances when, over a period of time, we lose our sense of connection with MIND (Spirit).

Whenever we lose contact with our true connection of life, the addiction to wrongful thinking/thoughts grows. This evolves into a harmful story that we support with our beliefs, and it eventually becomes a reality we have to live in. It's vital that we see that the spiritual and psychological worlds are One.

"Focus on the *missing link* between

our psychological nature and our spiritual nature."

*Reference:* **Todos Somos Uno (We All Are One)**

Powerful feelings of love were present in this talk with 25 Spanish-speaking participants from South America. Marina Galan translates my English into Spanish for the audience. <https://youtu.be/e7q7yj39OsQ>

# Chapter 6

## Summary of Chapters 1–5

- I like to say: *It's a Spiritual world. It's a world of* THOUGHT.

- In the 3P world, they might echo de Chardin, saying: *We are spiritual beings having a human experience.*

- Sydney Banks often talked about the "formless and the form being One." From the "Duality of Life" chapter of his *The Missing Link*:

  "As we start to regain the true relationship between our personal intelligence and the spiritual wisdom that lies within, we develop a higher degree of intelligence and common sense. This, in turn, clears up our misguided lives."

- Elsie Spittle, a pioneer 3P teacher and author of several books, sent this in an email to me:

  "The only correction is that I've never said my insight was about 'a thought creates a feeling.' What I've always shared is: 'THOUGHT creates feeling'. THOUGHT, as a Principle, is spiritual; the power to create. 'A thought' is a form of THOUGHT. 'A feeling' is a form of feeling. See the difference?"

- Dr. Dicken Bettinger, a prominent and popular 3P practitioner, psychologist, and author expressed in Aug 2017 in the "Addiction, Alcoholism & The 3 Principles" webinar series:

  "That's the cure for addiction. Experiencing the feeling of being One with life cures all that ails you. Long before we became addicted to substances, we became addicted, or caught up in, or identified with our own personal thinking. It becomes personal, it becomes egocentric, it's all about 'me.' When we fall wide open,

the personal mind goes to sleep. That's what Sydney Banks defined as meditative; our natural state is meditative."
<https://youtu.be/9iPaflLIwK4>

* * *

To summarize what I have tried to convey to the readers in the first five chapters:

1. The 3 Spiritual/Divine/Universal Principles of MIND, THOUGHT and CONSCIOUSNESS are the experience and understanding that eliminates all human suffering.

2. THOUGHT creates feeling.

3. Our past thoughts are illusions in time. They are only carried into the present moment via THOUGHT.

4. At one level of consciousness, our thoughts appear to control us. At another level, these antiquated thoughts are just ghosts passing through the night.

5. We are born innately healthy and habit-free. We are never broken.

# SECTION 2

# WHAT ARE THE PRINCIPLES?

# Chapter 7

# The 3 Principles

In one of my talks in Colombia, a participant asked if I could explain how CONSCIOUSNESS worked with MIND and THOUGHT. Through a translator, he said that he could understand the spiritual nature of CONSCIOUSNESS, but the other two were confusing to him. I said to him, cheekily, "I have the *perfecto* answer for you." He smiled, and I could see his undivided attention. I then said, "Read Sydney Banks's books and listen to his recordings. He is enlightened, and I am not, and there you will find the perfect answer to your question."

THE ULTIMATE ANSWER

SYDNEY BANKS

---

**Extracts from Sydney Banks's last talk just before he passed on in 2009**

---

The 3 Principles are a mental healing. They are an evolution. Whatever your teachers were taught and what you were taught was in absolute good faith and innocence, but now we are coming beyond that evolution to *a brand-new way* of looking at human behaviour.

**MIND** – Divine MIND is the intelligence of all things, whether in form or formless

**CONSCIOUSNESS** – is the Principle that allows us to see creation and all it entails

**THOUGHT** – is the Divine Gift that we use to go through life as thinking creatures

Anything that you add to that is what we do with our personal consciousness, and that will take you away from the truth.

As 3P therapists, you are telling people not to forget the past, but let them see that the past is an "illusion in time." The second you see that, you are free. There is no more garbage. Then you can look back in the past and laugh at it no matter what it was.

"MIND, CONSCIOUSNESS and THOUGHT

are the psychological trinity

of all human experience on earth.

They are the hidden pearls that lead us

to our true identity."

"Thought is the spiritual catalyst

that springs

MIND into action and

produces form."

Honestly, I could easily relay hundreds of Sydney Banks quotes, and they would all be applicable. So, my advice to readers is the same as to the Colombian participant above. Although truth is within, if one wants to understand truth, I suggest listening to or reading Sydney Banks's materials. They are priceless shrines of ancient and modern wisdom. What they are pointing to has grown and grown in my life.

Sydney Banks's words have changed me into a better human being and have provided me with a profounder understanding of who and what we all are.

**I love my life! You should love yours as well!**

# Chapter 8

## The Father of Modern Psychology

Psychology, in its present form, does not provide an explanation as to the source of feelings. It is obvious to me, as I experience these 3 Principles, that Sydney Banks has uncovered the missing link between spirit and psychology. He has, in the simplest of terms and concepts, answered the following cosmic puzzles:

a) What is the relationship between Universal MIND and personal mind? Are they as separate as they appear in our personal perception of life?

b) What is the role of THOUGHT in understanding the connection of the spiritual and material worlds? Must I be a victim of these personal and egotistical thoughts?

c) What is the relationship between Universal CONSCIOUSNESS and personal consciousness? How do we raise our level of awareness?

Human beings want to know about peace of mind, clarity, and living in a positive reality. Many have grown aware that there is a force or power beyond their intellect. What are the roles of religion, politics, social interaction and human morality in this world? Is it possible to change the world in its present condition, and can I contribute to this positive change? Even understanding the essence of religion brings up a need for clarity of heaven and hell, and how do I live in heaven here on earth?

The great thing is that all of these and the thousands of other questions about life are 100 percent answered by the 3 Principles—MIND, THOUGHT and CONSCIOUSNESS. Of course, if one thinks about it, how can it not be, when these 3 Principles are the originator and composition of these questions. We simply have to go to the source of the question to find the answer; so when Sydney Banks says they are the ultimate answer to solving all suffering within humanity (which includes addiction), he is not kidding.

## A Few Personal Observations about the 3 Principles

In my view, the 3 Principles, as uncovered by Sydney Banks, are the ultimate answer to addiction. First, human beings want to stop the pattern of self-destruction; and, second, they want to uncover the love inside their being. Voilà, the answer lies in truth, and the understanding of the 3 Principles leads everyone, regardless of outside negative circumstances or past experiences, to truth.

*Can one become free of addiction without an awareness of the 3 Principles?*

Of course! The answer lies in truth, whether one experiences truth by playing golf, or through the messages of Christ, Buddha, Mohammed, Bill W. or anyone else. Healing is healing! Yet, even if one is unaware of it, the healing is created via the 3 Principles.

Here are a few interesting questions to contemplate. How can I write about the 3 Principles when I do not fully understand them? How can I write about something that is impossible to grasp intellectually? How am I brave enough to try to describe formlessness, emptiness and silence? If the Principles are spiritual and formless yet create all of life as we see it, how does one become a teacher of the 3 Principles? And even more puzzling, how does one even know these Principles exist when they are shapeless, spiritual tools that the formless energy of everything uses to create form. This is very confusing to the intellect.

I know they exist because I have experienced various insights that illuminate their existence, their power, and what they point to. I cannot explain this in words, I simply love that the Principles are there to

36

guide me in a psychologically sane manner. I want to be happy and content in my life. These are the tools that chisel out the perfect statue, moment to moment to moment. And if the statue is messed up via insecure or fearful thinking, they are the tools that point me back inside to where sanity and peace of mind exist.

I have one more ace up my sleeve: Sydney Banks, who in his enlightened state of consciousness, uncovered these three precious and sacred Principles. Whenever I need guidance, his words, videos, books, CDs are just as alive for me as when he first recorded them. They are here for eternity to guide us. They are pure knowledge. The wisdom within his materials is eternal. You do not require anything else in order to recognize the spiritual nature of who you are! And we do not need anything in order to understand that these 3 Principles are our true nature. They are us, we are them.

The purity of Sydney Banks's message leaves us on very solid ground. We do not need any other material, and he would say that we do not even need his material, for the answer always lies inside our soul or consciousness. All we have to do is experience this *as a fact*; then life will never be the same, and we will never see life with the same eyes. It will be as if we are born anew with a brand-new way of seeing life.

**This process is continual, with no beginning and ending—it just is.**

SECTION 3

RESPECTING ALL APPROACHES

TO

ADDICTION AND ALCOHOLISM

They have and are contributing to the evolution!

# Chapter 9

## Bill Wilson and the 12-Step Programs

Many may wonder why I discuss 12-Step programs when I am neither a teacher nor proponent of them. To me, the answer is obvious—they cannot be ignored. No matter how persuasively, throughout my career, I have talked about the wisdom of the Principles in the addiction world, there have always been gentle confrontations with clients because of their exposure to and understanding of the 12 Steps. I, too, initially experienced bewilderment regarding these two different approaches, so I am assuming this may also be the case for some readers. Certainly, Bill W. offered something substantial, and the 12 Steps cannot be simply dismissed with an attitude of "my approach is better than you.

Let us take a skeleton look at Bill W. and the 12 Steps.

---

### Obituary excerpt from the New York Times
(two underlined subheads added by the author)

## Bill W., Dies; Cofounder of Alcoholics Anonymous

Jan. 27, 1971 – New York Times News Service

NEW YORK – William Griffith Wilson died late Sunday night and, with the announcement of his death, was revealed to have been the Bill W. who cofounded Alcoholics Anonymous in 1935. He was 75.

The retired Wall Street securities analyst had expected to die or to go insane as a hopeless drunk 36 years ago but—after what he called a dramatic spiritual experience—sobered up and stayed sober.

He leaves a program of recovery as a legacy to 47,000 acknowledged alcoholics in 15,000 A.A. groups throughout the United States and in 18 other countries.

## HIS EXPERIENCE

Bill W. found himself crying out:

"If there is a God, let him show himself, I am ready to do anything, anything!"

"Suddenly," he related. "the room lit up with a great white light. I was caught up into an ecstasy which there are no words to describe. It seemed that a wind not of air but of spirit was blowing. And then it burst upon me that I was a free man."

Recovering slowly and fired with enthusiasm, Mr. Wilson envisioned a chain reaction among drunks, one carrying the message of recovery to the next. Emphasizing at first his spiritual regeneration, and working closely with Oxford Groupers, he struggled for months to "sober up the world," but got almost nowhere.

## IS ADDICTION A DISEASE?

Mr. Wilson thereafter concentrated on the basic philosophy that alcoholism is a physical allergy coupled with a mental obsession—an incurable though arrestable—illness of body, mind and spirit. Much later, the disease concept of alcoholism was accepted by a committee of the American Medical Association and by the World Health Organization.

I believe this is a true story. The renowned Swiss psychiatrist Carl Jung was helping a client with addiction when this client had a spiritual awakening, which immediately cured him of alcoholism. The client then met one of his former drinking buddies who asked what had happened. The cured client told his friend about his spiritual awakening, and the friend, too, became cured. This second man met up with another alcoholic friend, who, again, asked "What happened?" The sharing of the spiritual insight led to this man also having a spiritual insight. That third man was Bill W., which probably explains why, in the story to follow, he wanted to talk with Carl Jung.

Joe Bailey, a seasoned 3P Practitioner and psychologist specializing in addiction, related the following to me at the Three Principles Global Community conference in Los Angeles (2016):

> Bill W. would have loved Sydney Banks, if Bill had been alive in 1973, which was when Syd had his enlightenment experience.
>
> When Bill W. was at the beginning of his journey, there were three major psychological approaches: Freud, Adler and Jung. Carl Jung was the most spiritual of the three, and when Bill W. talked to Jung, this is what the famous psychologist told him. First, Jung stated that he had never seen psychotherapy be effective in addiction. As far as he could see, there were three paths that did work with addiction. The first path was through a spiritual awakening or a revelation via a deep religious experience. The second was if someone experienced a spiritual awakening or an insight in a non-religious manner (similar to Sydney Banks's experience). The third way was to truly see "what MIND is."
>
> After Sydney Banks had his spiritual experience, he shared how others could uncover this understanding of "what MIND is," or as he later defined it, the 3 Principles."

It certainly would have been interesting to be a fly on the wall if these three gentlemen, Carl Jung, Bill W., and Sydney Banks, had been able to have a discussion together.

### A Few Personal Observations about Spiritual Insight and A.A.

a) In my opinion, Bill W.'s spiritual insight proves that any ordinary person can, at any moment, or over time, experience the spiritual answer for addiction, and remain alcohol-free for the rest of their lives.

I have the deepest respect for the depth of Bill W.'s revelation. His teachings and contributions continue to help many people who are addicted. I also believe that, because of his spiritual and religious message, A.A. achieved much higher results in its earlier years. As the 12-Steps evolved over time, it seems to have lost some of the spiritual essence (even though *many* might argue against this statement, since A.A. has saved their lives or has been their major support system).

b) Regarding the obituary notice, I added the subheading "Is Addiction a Disease?" in order to suggest the possibility of an evolution to the status quo understandings of the disease model of A.A.

- Bill Wilson explained in 1960 why A.A. had refrained from using the term *disease*, saying:

"We A.A.s have never called alcoholism a disease because, technically speaking, it is not a disease entity. For example, there is no such thing as heart disease. Instead, there are many separate heart ailments or combinations of them. It is something like that with alcoholism. Therefore, we did not wish to get in wrong with the medical profession by pronouncing alcoholism a disease entity. Hence, we have always called it an illness or a malady—a far safer term for us to use."

- In the early 1970s, the term *disease* became accepted by the United Nations. This helped raise public awareness that law enforcement and imprisonment was not the only alternative to helping those who are addicted.

The 12-Step fellowships, in their most generalized understanding, define *addiction* and *alcoholism* as threefold illnesses: a physical allergy, a mental obsession and a spiritual malady.

- The Big Book states that alcoholism "is an illness which only a spiritual experience will conquer."

Ernest Kurtz, whose doctoral dissertation was published as *Not-God: A History of Alcoholics Anonymous*, stated that this is "the closest the book *Alcoholics Anonymous* comes to a definition of *alcoholism*."

- **Portugal** has been a leader in dismissing the disease model and in looking at addiction as a personal health issue. Since it decriminalized all drugs in 2001, Portugal has seen dramatic drops in overdoses, HIV infection and drug-related crime. "Portugal's policy rests on three pillars: one, that there's no such thing as a soft or hard drug, only healthy and unhealthy relationships with drugs; two, that an individual's unhealthy relationship with drugs often conceals frayed relationships with loved ones, with the world around them, and with themselves; and three, that the eradication of all drugs is an impossible goal. The national policy is to treat each individual differently," Dr. Goulão (a doctor specializing in treating drug addiction) . . . [said], "The secret is for us to be present."

- https://www.theguardian.com/news/2017/dec/05/portugals-radical-drugs-policy-is-working-why-hasnt-the-world-copied-it

c) In my opinion, Sydney Banks's spiritual insight demonstrates that any ordinary person can experience the full healing power of the Spirit in just a few seconds and become enlightened.

The 3 Principles teaches that we are always healthy—it is a health model—while the 12 Steps evolved into a disease model in the 1970s. What Bill W. came to offer was a godsend and a vessel of hope for people who are addicted. However, it is <u>not true</u> that people who are addicted are *powerless* against addiction. In fact, I have seen that there are many ex-alcoholics or ex-addicted who experienced healing in A.A. or other programs, and who have evolved past a definition of disease into seeing that their condition was a bad habit that they had left behind.

Let's be clear about what I am saying here. Higher power or spiritual MIND will always be the answer to addiction, whether we are aware of it or not. Consequently, once we have experienced the healing energy of MIND, we are healed and will see/experience a brave new world, especially if our understanding includes the true nature of THOUGHT as it relates to addiction.

Holding onto the false, but innocent, thought that we are diseased for the rest of our lives is psychologically detrimental to our ongoing mental health. Carrying or projecting a thought forward through time is as damaging as believing an externally imposed label, such as when we are told we are "the stupidest person in the world." We are not these thoughts or labels, but if we believe a false label, we will falsely identify ourselves with it. That is the power of beliefs. That is the power of THOUGHT.

Labels point us in the wrong direction. Whether in school, the workforce or general life, a negative label is one of the most harmful forces in our society today. Labels lead to prejudice, injustice, gossip and many more detrimental results. We are born pure, and that stays with us for eternity. We are born habit-free. We need to know this.

d) What has impressed me about Bill W. and A.A., seeing as that I am not an expert in either? Besides the *fellowship of support*, I resonate with four phrases that are in the Big Book. They are:

*higher power*

*stinky thinking*

*authentic self*

*spiritual awakening*

To me, these ideas point all people in a positive and helpful direction.

"MIND, CONSCIOUSNESS and THOUGHT are the psychological trinity

of all human experience on earth.

They are the hidden pearls that lead us to our true identity."


**And, I will add, they are the cure to addiction.**

# ADDENDUM to this Chapter

## Some Data:

a) Present-day sobriety statistics (as of October 2018) are much lower

**Sobriety Statistics for the Pioneers of Alcoholics Anonymous**
**1934 to 1939**

| Total Count | Sober | Continuous Sobriety Unknown |
|---|---|---|
| 77 (100%) | 40 (52%) | 37 (48%) |

- https://bigbooksponsorship.org/articles-alcoholism-addiction-12-step-program-recovery/fellowship/sobriety-statistics-12-step-recovery-rates/

b) The simplest explanation is that 12-Step treatment and A.A. meetings work for some people but not for others. J. Scott Tonigan, a researcher at the University of New Mexico Center on Alcoholism, Substance Abuse, and Addictions (CASAA), said that research indicates: About a third of people maintain recovery from alcohol addiction as a result of 12-Step treatment, another third get something out of the treatment but not enough for full recovery, and another third get nothing at all.

c) Dr. Lance Dodes, in his 2014 book, *The Sober Truth*, argues that most people who have experienced A.A. have not achieved long-term sobriety. He makes the controversial argument that research indicates that only 5 to 8 percent of the people who attend one or more A.A. meetings achieve sobriety for longer than one year. In a

2015 article for *The Atlantic* magazine, Gabrielle Glaser used Dodes's figures to argue that A.A. has a low success rate.

d) My own observations of the world of addiction also suggest that the recovery rate is low.

## Conclusion

Obviously, Bill W. contributed greatly to the understanding of the world in the field of addiction and its evolvement into Alcoholics Anonymous and other similar organizations. It is possible that some of what Bill W. experienced may have been misconstrued in its evolvement. It is also possible that Bill W. did not understand everything about addiction, and that he used his personal thinking to fill in those areas in which he was unclear. In fact, I might be so bold to say that if Bill W. were alive today, he would likely contribute new insights that would further the positive evolvement of A.A. and magnify its impact in the field of addiction.

For me, that is the innocence of being a human being. We do not understand everything, and we evolve. Many times, in our attempt to share a spiritual insight, we veer in our language from the purity and simplicity of that insight we receive. It follows, then, that whatever we think or add with our personal mind are not principles.

The 3 Principles point us back to whence we came before we created the mess. When we get back on track, this is where we will uncover the *ultimate answer* to our self-created mess.

# Chapter 10

## The Collision of the Indigenous World and Addiction

In many ways, this chapter was one of the most challenging, yet rewarding to write. As I am non-Indigenous, no matter the words or tone I use, my writing may be judged and criticized by some. If I offend anyone in my desire to share what I have seen, please know it is not written with that intent.

I originally went into the Indigenous world to help the suffering of their people. I sometimes have experienced difficulty knowing how to integrate or understand the customs, mannerisms and protocols of these fine people. What I did accomplish over time was to be friends with many, and to be accepted by some.

*I split this chapter in two. If you find Part A too difficult to follow, simply skip to Part B. Part A is written primarily for the Indigenous perspective and those familiar with that culture. Part B is for a general audience.*

### PART A: If You Say It, It Must Be Substantiated With Story

Even choosing what to call the Indigenous has been a journey. When I began working with them in the 1990s, they called themselves "Indian." The Elders still continue to use the term. Then "Indian" became politically incorrect, and labels like "Native" and "Aboriginal" came into usage, but the Indigenous classified these as "White Man words" or "government words." "First Nations" and "First People" became popular in Canada but not worldwide. Now "Indigenous" is popular, but, to me, it sounds too bookish, and I could not even spell it correctly at first.

Many of the Indigenous are proud of their own ideas, and while understanding that all humans have the same color of blood, they can at times be sensitive or prejudicial. The past injustices they have been exposed to has much to do with this.

Among the Indigenous, there is an inconsistency of spiritual teachings which leads to conflict and confusion, often leaving many feeling left out or separated from the whole. Gossip and jealousy are possibly the top negative influences within the culture of Indigenous communities.

Nonetheless, I love this culture and its people. They are loving and caring, and their kindness, generosity and goodwill has led me to become a better human being. Their love of family and honoring of spirit is powerful, and I have been privileged to be allowed inside their world. I would like to share a bit of my journey:

\* \* \*

I am proud of my Indigenous Spirit name—Standing Elk—given to me by Black Thunderbird Man (aka John Delorme). It has been my honor to work and/or be involved with numerous Indigenous organizations, ceremonies and communities for more than two decades (as of this writing), and I believe some of my understanding of the Indigenous world is rooted in this book. However, I was not born Indigenous and do not pretend to fully understand what it is to think or live, in this world, as an Indigenous person. Certainly, I have heard the stories, the travesties of justice regarding the Indigenous plight with respect to residential schools, colonization, being classified as "savages"; and the many instances of White people pretending they know what is best for the Indigenous People. These stories always touch my heart, evoke my compassion and make me aware that I have not lived them; that I have simply heard the "crying and prayers of a nation" as an outsider.

The above is a paraphrase of these feelings in my 2010 book, Alita's Sacred Journey.

Now, in 2019, I am considered by some as an Elder, a man of the Spirit who is the carrier of a Tonka pipe and woman's medicine. This pipe was carved in 2008 from a block of pipestone that came from the only sacred mountain in the United States, by a brother and master carver incarcerated in a Nevada maximum-security prison. The bowl of the pipe was carved, using solely a stone and a nail, into a sacred buffalo; and the pipe was passed on to Flying Climbing Squirrel (aka Larry Petersen) in a sacred prison ceremony where three pipes were being initiated. This was the head pipe in the ceremony.

A few years later, around 2010, Flying Climbing Squirrel mailed this pipe to me, because it was his Lakota tradition to give away his most sacred possession to the person who had greatly uplifted his soul and spirit. Perhaps, Spirit had guided him to send this precious gift. The day the parcel arrived from the Nevada prison with the pipe, a beautiful decorated feather, a stuffed spider and teachings from Flying Climbing Squirrel written on lined foolscap, was the day I began my journey as a pipe carrier, and I initially wondered why I was chosen.

On the foolscap, he had written: "I am truly grateful you accepted the pipe into your heart and life, and yes, Harry, the pipe will truly guide you in some very profound experiences providing you remain open. I have found in prison that, at times, remaining open becomes very difficult because an awakened pipe's purpose is to guide us to the suffering so that we may bring peace in those lives. There is a lot of suffering in prison. Out there, I imagine there is as well. So, use this sacred tool as your guide, and with your already deep wisdom you will surely be able to alleviate much suffering."

That day, I entered into a new relationship with all the Indigenous People, one which allowed me to talk to their hearts. The pipe has continued to create a closer connection to the People, and it has permitted me to grow in a more natural way with the Indigenous world than before. The role of the pipe is ceremonial. What it carries is spiritual.

It is extremely rare for any man to carry women's medicine, yet it came to me, and this has generated wonderful effects, allowing many

Indigenous women to release their deepest emotions and feelings. And when freed, they naturally connect to the Great Spirit or Oneness this book often refers to. The woman's medicine is called "Bear's Weed" or "the Sacred Herb," and one burns it to nurture and protect that which is ancient, sacred and wild within oneself.

In its own mysterious way, Spirit pointed to three plants on the ground as I was walking up a mountain in Nevada's Red Rock Canyon National Conservation Area. It was in late November, with a little snow on the ground, which is the only time this medicine is fresh and fully potent. The three plants were Bear's Weed, Black brush and Nevada Juniper. As the answers came, I grew to understand Black brush as the male balancing plant, which allows men to experience the Bear's Weed without being overpowered by its feminine influence. Nevada Juniper has no medicinal contribution in this particular mixture; it merely adds to the smell and presentation of the medicine.

The pipe I carry prays to the 7 Sacred Directions that are identified in the Medicine Wheel. These are the union between the 4 Directions and the 3 Spiritual Principles of Creation. Indigenous teachings highlight the Four Directions (i.e., West, South, East and North as expressing the spiritual, emotional, physical and mental worlds). These directions express the emanations of Spirit in their entirety, or what Mother Earth has created in union with Father Sky (or, as South American spiritual Elders would say, "What Mother Moon has created in union with Father Sun").

The Father and Mother along with the 7th direction, the Spirit inside every human, are the trinity of Native spirituality. The Father is the masculine force that is expressed through the feminine power of the Mother. At the deepest part of the Mother and Father, where they are connected, lies the Origin of Thought. This was taught to me by a member of the Coast Salish medicine women.

When our power within connects with the Father and Mother, we have the perfect manifestation of the physical and psychological worlds (i.e., the Four Directions). The three primary forces—the 5th, 6th and 7th directions—create the perfect expression of life.

"We are the babies of the stars, our star relatives, ascending to the most powerful shamanic teachings from Peru, Los Andes. The 7 dimensions embodied us into beings—above, underground, in front, behind us, left side, right side and within. Our relatives are based upon these elements wherever you turn, or take actions." —written by Marcella Loyer (description below).

All the major religions have the truth. So, in Christianity we have the 3 Principles of religion (the Father, the Son, and the Holy Spirit); from Sydney Banks, we have the 3 Principles of psychology (Mind, Thought and Consciousness); and from White Calf Woman, who is often seen as the originator of Native spirituality, we have the 3 Principles of Native spirituality (Father Sky, Mother Earth, and the Spirit within). All three describe the perfection and oneness of life. Now, it is true that no one else is talking about the 3 Principles of Native spirituality, but my insight comes from Spirit and is pure.

Furthermore, Spirit has given me additional teachings that are perfect for my walk in the Indigenous world. Maybe not for others, but for me it has worked! I have been required to learn to be myself through what I have been exposed to in the combined worlds of the 3 Principles and Native spirituality. Both worlds emphasize the "spiritual essence of being who you are," and both worlds point to "silence that teaches", rather than just spoken words. This silence is where I found my understanding of True Self, that which I have been fortunate to experience.

As I have grown truer to myself, my understanding of what the Indigenous People are expressing with their hearts, words and actions has grown. I do not profess an ability to describe a collective Indigenous feeling, but, from what I see, I can describe what it is like to be in the Indigenous bubble of life. These teachings have allowed me to "do my best, and allow Spirit to do the rest."

Marcella Loyer (a Chiricahua Apache/Mexican Indian, with Sicilian blood, whose father was born in Camp Verde, Arizona; one of the great-granddaughters of Geronimo, whose blood lineage includes both Mexico and the United States; and author of Credo for the American Indian Movement (A.I.M.) International: Chapters and Divisions on a Worldwide Level) once told me, "Wars, conflicts, and jealousy of tribe leaders and nations resulting in clashes had occurred long before the encounters with the White man, their government, and clergy. Territorial fights, murders of tribal leaders or chiefs, priests, along with the common Indigenous Peoples fighting for total control of bloodlines and territories, were always there in the Americas."

Also, in her Apache teachings, she emphasizes that "the origins of the Native cultures in the Americas was taught by our true ancestors from South American countries, from Central America to Mexico . . . from the Incan, Mayan, Aztec, Toltec, and Olmec civilizations. Our observatories for the skies; our knowledge of the supernatural worlds; forces in astronomy, physics, mathematics that led to the creation of the Mayan calendar, and their predictions of the end of the world as we live it today because of the human sickness of the mind! . . . We need to know about the Theory of Evolution that we endorse along with Charles Darwin and Jane Goodall in relation to nature, our close animal relatives and the universal forces of all life."

What seems obvious from Marcella's statements is that her fine People were by no means unwise, nor were they perfect. Yet, they suffered greatly at the hands of the 'white people' and their thinking and actions. The amount of trauma experienced within this culture as a whole is huge, and, as you can imagine, being traumatized is often one of the psychological barriers that contribute to being heavily addicted. In the case of the Indigenous, they have experienced trauma individually and collectively. And yet, they are still rising! And they are evolving.

# A Sacred Moment in Time

*If life was a stream, there would be no oceans.*
*If life was an ocean, there would be no rivers.*

*In troubled times, we lose perspective of where we are.*
*In confused times, we look for clarity*
*In mysterious times, we search for simplicity.*

*Finally, we SEE*
*We are the stream, the ocean and the river*
*We are perspective, clarity and simplicity.*

*Standing Elk*

\* \* \*

**PART B: Freedom From Addiction**

Beyond the old stereotypical images, there are a growing number of well-educated Indigenous People. Brilliant minds that are sensitive to the injustices of this world. Canada's National Centre for Truth and Reconciliation Commission has published its conclusions about some of these extensive changes in attitude regarding the injustice and prejudice of the government, police, helping professions, and general Canadian population. The Indigenous want the injustice to be acknowledged, and they want to heal from their inhumane tragedies. They believe this will enable them to prosper within the social structures of the great nations of Canada and the United States.

The movie *Spotlight* (Academy Award® winner for Best Picture, 2016) highlights the true story of how the *Boston Globe* uncovered the massive scandal of child molestation and cover-up within the local Catholic Archdiocese, shaking the entire Catholic Church to its core.

The movie accurately depicts the guilt, disgust and trauma experienced by the molested children. The child molestation depicted in the movie is mild in comparison to what Indigenous children experienced in Residential Schools. Payout by the Canadian government for the injustice to the 86,000 Natives attending residential schools will surpass $3-4 billion CAD when completed. Phrases like "the forced assimilations by rape, destruction of our children" could also be added to the justification for why the payout is so large.

Many non-Indigenous have asked me, "If Indigenous People are so spiritually gifted, why do they experience so many psychological problems, and alcoholism and drug addiction?" (see Steve Adair and Harry (Standing Elk) on "the sacred feeling of Native spirituality and the 3 Principles," in the YouTube series *Hope & Challenges - Three Principles in Action in Denmark* for a partial answer.
<https://www.youtube.com/watch?v=KSavawGMwh0&t=84s>

It needs to be acknowledged that the Indigenous walk of life, including Indigenous ceremony, help many of their People in healing their internal conflicts with addiction, prison and general life. While it is true that there are still many Indigenous with addiction problems, it is a powerful statement to say that more Indigenous have left the addiction world than any other culture, and many are living fruitful and spiritual existences.

One interesting phenomenon is that this shedding of addiction has been most prevalent among shamans and spiritual healers. They were the easiest to be seduced by the evil brew called "crazywater" (that which stole their spirit); yet they were the most influential and wisest when returning from that burned-out world to the world of helping others. They never lost their Ancient Wisdom or spirit power; they simply put them on hold while they were living in hiatus.

I have been given permission to share the following story honoring the Black Horse Spirit. When told, it included the awe or wonderment of a story carried from seven generations past, and it was told in the fashion of sharing in the oral tradition of Indigenous storytelling. Chief Thunderbird Child (aka Kenny Awasis), whose Cree teachings come from the Old Ways of the People handed down from Elder to Elder, expressed this story:

In a sacred sweat lodge ceremony in 2018, Chief Thunderbird Child said he would call in the Black Horse Spirit to help a group of seven who were looking for healing, as they were in a 12-Step recovery program for substance abuse. It was their good luck and wisdom that they had decided to participate in this sweat and pipe ceremony. Chief Thunderbird Child talked lovingly of how calling upon the Black Horse Spirit would guide those to lose their urge for alcohol or other addictive substance, for it was the mystical gift of the Black Horse Spirit.

He told an ancient story of an Indian who needed to go a long, long distance in a very short period of time. The Indian got on a black horse and took off for miles and miles into the distance. The heat was extreme, and after many, many hours, the horse's legs gave out, and it stumbled forward with back legs up but front legs folded under themselves on the ground. The rider got off the horse and searched all over his saddle until he found a canteen. He fed the full contents of the canteen to the horse as this was where the need was the greatest. This rejuvenated the horse, and they made it to their destination.

That night, there was a sweat ceremony, and the Indian rider participated in order to celebrate his good luck in making it there under troubled conditions. The Black Horse Spirit (a mystical horse that, to the Indian eye, is as real as any physical horse) appeared in the middle of the ceremony and told this story. The Horse said the contents of the canteen saved his life, and it was the generosity and compassion of the Indian rider that also saved his life. He then surprised the participants of the sweat by saying that the canteen was full of whiskey. Even though it was not water, it saved his life, and because of that he was able to make it to their destination. Because of the consideration of this Indian Rider, the Black Horse wanted to help humankind save itself from the allure and seduction of being addicted to alcohol, so it is passing on its Spirit to stop and eliminate the urge of alcohol.

The power of this Spirit came into our lodge, and for many the urge vanished. Unfortunately, for most, their urge would later reignite, mainly because they did not fully grasp the role of THOUGHT. Old thoughts and memories from the past were re-creating the urge—if they thought the same old thoughts that they walked into the lodge with, the urge would return and continue to haunt their dreams and lives. Holding onto old beliefs is very seductive. Yet, because of the spiritual power of these ceremonies, many are uplifted into a hope-filled future. Those who aren't, however, will have to find another way.

"The wise medicine men in the Native North American culture

spoke of the world as **one** spirit,

referring to the creator of all things as the '**Great Spirit**'.

This was their way of explaining the oneness of life."

The 3 Principles are the essence of all beginnings. Great Spirit or Divine MIND needs spiritual tools to create form. These spiritual tools are Spirit (MIND), THOUGHT and CONSCIOUSNESS. They are the building blocks of all ideas, cultures, organizations, religions and everything else. Native spirituality, just like Christianity, Buddhism, Islam, and Hinduism, is an expression of the Spirit.

How old is Native spirituality? They say it has been here from the beginning of time, and that all humans are indigenous to Mother Earth. Before form is original medicine. Here lies the origin or root of healing of addiction.

The 3 Principles, to my way of seeing, also reveal the portal to this original medicine. The 3 Principles have the power to assist all travellers, Indigenous or others, to uncover the great mystery of the universe. This uncovering is the truth of "who we are." This connection not only heals addiction, it heals the entirety of you. In my opinion, addiction is only a symptom for human beings trying to escape a victim story. This cloak of beliefs they are wearing is tremendously heavy. Understanding the role of THOUGHT in this puzzle lightens the load.

\* \* \*

Before speaking at a breakout group at the 2018 3PUK Conference in London—where more than 1,000 attended the entire event—I was invited by Rabbi Shaul Rosenblatt to his home for a Shabbat lunch along with twenty other Jews. It was a very enjoyable time, full of beautiful feelings and delicious food. I happened to overhear the rabbi express the following to a leading psychiatrist also attending this holy time: "The more I learn about the 3 Principles, the more I understand the Ancient Wisdom of Judaism. And just as powerful, the more I have an insight into the wisdom of Judaism, the more I understand the 3 Principles."

I have had a similar experience in regard to Native spirituality and the 3 Principles. And I have never asked why Native spirituality chose me.

**Indigenous see Spirit in Everything, whether in form or formless.**

**Reference:** www.acttraining.biz (From the home page, download the collaborative paper written by Melinda Eagle Kline, Jonathan Couchman and Harry "Standing Elk," titled, "The Three Principles and Native Spirituality.")

# Chapter 11

## Religion, Mindfulness and Addiction

Many of the addicted are religious. I love the support their religions give the mind and heart. While it is not my way—I am spiritual, not religious—I recognize the power of truth within all the major religions of our world.

In a class at the Recovery Centre where I taught the Principles, there was an Iranian chap who possessed a strong understanding of Mohammed and his teachings. I mentioned to him that in the Kabbalah of the Judaic religion, they called God "The Great Nothingness." I asked him what the Muslim world might say. He paused for a moment, and then said, "Emptiness." Besides talking about praying five times a day and surrendering to Allah, he mentioned the word *fitrah*, which means "natural innate disposition" or "instinctual." I mentioned that in the 3 Principles we have the same phrase, except that we call it "innate mental health" or "innate wisdom."

In the Native book *Fools Crow: Wisdom and Power* (by Thomas E. Mails, Council Oaks Books, 1991, pp. 30-31), Spirit is expressed through the metaphor of "hollowness."

> The great holy man, Black Elk, said, "I cured with the power that came through me. Of course, it was not I who cured. It was the power from the outer world, and the visions and ceremonies had only made me like a hole through which the power could come to the two-leggeds. If I thought that I was doing it myself, the hole would close up and no power could come through. Then everything I could do would be foolish." . . .
>
> "We (Black Elk and [Fools Crow]) talked about this several times. We agreed that the Higher Powers had taught us this same thing. We are *just holes*. But as I have

63

used hollow bones for curing, I have decided that it is better to think of medicine people as little hollow bones."

. . .

"In and through. The power comes to us first to make us what we should be, and then flows through us and out to others."

## CHRISTIANITY

Christianity, of course, has been a global provider of spiritual sustenance. In the world of addiction, by itself and in combination with 12-Step programs, Christianity is a major player.

A Christian woman, who wished to remain anonymous, once told me:

When you are looking at true Christianity, what you are looking at is "who you truly are" in God. Therefore, it is important to understand that what you receive is not from formal religion, it comes from Divine MIND. Understanding from here is where you need to hear from, not from the already manifested.

Alcoholism is not a disease as we think it is; rather it is us not utilizing who we truly are in God. We create a reality that seems real, so real that to go beyond it seems impossible. In truth, the reality that is created is not of God, and therefore it is false. For our origin is forged in God. Here is the knowledge that is required to have anyone go past addiction—to be who we truly are in God. Life then becomes a true joy simply to be alive.

To me, Christians are often angels who share the gift of life with the needy and underprivileged. They provide food, shelter and spiritual sustenance for the homeless, addicted and mentally dysfunctional. However, there are many instances when the actions of Christians have proven regrettable. A simple example was presented at a Haida Gwaii exhibit at the Museum of Vancouver. As stated on their presentation materials: "The Potlach Ban of 1884 and other Colonial impositions such as Christianity prevented the carvings and raising of monumental poles (totem poles) for decades."

In the world of addiction, Christianity has had many success stories that cannot be denied. Originally, when A.A. had its highest success rates, it was fully interfaced with Christianity. In this modern era, Christianity is still a major player in the 12-Step programs, but many A.A. programs take educational and spiritual sustenance from other sources as well.

### Brief History of A.A. and Christianity

Alcoholics Anonymous (A.A.), the first 12-Step fellowship, was founded in 1935 in Akron, Ohio, by Bill Wilson and Dr. Robert Holbrook Smith, known to A.A. members as "Bill W." and "Dr. Bob". When he was alive, Dr. Bob insisted on Christian-based practices to be integrated at all times within A.A. He died in 1950.

From *Alcoholics Anonymous Comes of Age* (Alcoholics Anonymous World Services, Incorporated, 1973, p. 162): "The story of how the first three A.A.s got sober is not a story about an A.A. program. It is an account of how three down-and-out Christian alcoholics—who believed in God, had been Bible students, and had been active in churches at a one or more points in their lives—admitted their alcoholism, determined to quit for good, turned to God for help, were cured, and actively helped others for the rest of their days. Then came Bill Wilson's 'new version of the program . . . the 12 Steps.'"

These two quotes highlight an aspect of Bill W. and Dr. Bob's Christian views:

> *Bill W.*: "An alcoholic is a fellow who is 'trying to get his religion out of a bottle' when what he really wants is unity within himself, unity with God . . ."

> *Dr. Bob*: "It wasn't until 1938 that the teachings and efforts and stories that had been going on were crystallized in the form of the 12 Steps. I didn't write the 12 Steps. I had nothing to do with the writing of them. We already had the basic ideas, though not in terse and tangible form. We got them, as I said, as a result of our study of the Good Book [i.e., the Bible]." (*The Co-Founders of Alcoholics Anonymous: Biographical Sketches: Their Last Major Talks*, p. 14.)

As I've came to understand it, the first actual A.A. program was Bible-based. It had no 12 Steps or 12 Traditions. It had no Big Book. And it had no "war stories" or meetings like those seen today. These pioneers believed the answers to their problems were in the Bible. They called themselves a "Christian fellowship."

From Dick B's website <dickb.com/index.html> and his account of A.A.'s history:

> "In his personal evolution, Bill W. prepared his Big Book and the content of his "Steps" from knowledge he borrowed from Dr. William D. Silkworth, Professor William James, and Reverend Samuel M. Shoemaker, Jr. You will note how **A.A. moved from its original quest for a Bible-based cure of alcoholism by the power of God to self-made 12-Steps drawn from the above-named philosopher, psychiatrist, and Episcopalian Rector.**"

What I have hoped to document is that A.A. has changed or evolved over the years, as has Christianity's influence on its programs, although some may disagree. Christianity's influence in the spiritual development of human beings is substantial today, but it is somewhat less than in 1935. Christ's message of a "higher power," which Bill W. often voiced, is undeniable. There is also an irrefutable truth—if a person who is addicted experiences a revelation, insight or vision that is God-based, this will change a human being forever.

## MINDFULNESS

While I am not knowledgeable about mindfulness, I see it as a partial evolvement in treating addiction and alcoholism. To my way of seeing, it leads one to take a look at the power that lies within and in the power of Now. On the YouTube series *Addiction, Alcoholism & The 3 Principles*, I suggest that mindfulness appears to sit at the entrance of the subject of CONSCIOUSNESS.

Mindfulness is a practice in which one learns to quiet the mind by focusing on the present activity/moment in which one is living—be it doing those dishes or sitting still. One exercise to practice is mindful eating. For this, take a piece of fruit or even a piece of chocolate bar and hold it in your hand. Explore it with all five senses. Look it over, smell it, and use your fingers to really feel the textures of the fruit. Then, place it in your mouth. Notice how it feels on your tongue, the saliva building in your mouth and the way that it tastes. Notice the moment that you bite into it—how does it feel? What distinct flavors can you taste? This simple exercise is the basis of mindfulness, being completely focused on the present moment, focusing on the tastes and flavors, and quieting all other thoughts. In the same way that you can quiet your thoughts while eating, the theory goes, you can quiet your reactive thoughts when you encounter a stressor.

In mindfulness theory, stressors—outside events or emotional human reactions that cause stress—are everywhere around us. We live in a world where we are constantly connected to news that focuses on trauma and upset. We feel the need to be constantly moving and constantly available via phone, text, email, etc. When a person experiences one of these stressful situations, the body releases hormones as a response to danger. Prolonged or acute stress often facilitates a relapse of addiction.

From what I have come to understand, mindfulness emphasizes personal triggers and stress as two major causes of relapse. And while it may be somewhat easy for a recovering addict to avoid going to bars or hanging out with people they used with before getting sober, it's harder to avoid stress. Mindfulness is the practice of cultivating nonjudgmental awareness in day-to-day life. It means being fully aware of what is happening in the present moment without filters or judgement. By practicing mindfulness meditation, we can possibly train the brain to consciously accept the stressors that we experience in day-to-day life and deal with them in a calm and positive way.

Mindfulness practitioners view those who have become dependent on drugs or alcohol as living their lives in a reactive state, usually letting their thoughts dictate their actions and experiences. Mindfulness programs suggest to clients that mindfulness-based practices allow humans to become more aware of their thoughts, sensations and situations. Clients can then make good decisions and act appropriately with more purpose, compassion and understanding.

The 3 Principles teachings are now contributing to the world of addiction. Principles-based programs and various individual 3P practitioners have achieved many successes in the field of addiction. Some 3 Principles programs and facilities offer a non-12-Step holistic drug-rehab program that goes beyond addiction and promotes a new outlook on life. Several of these programs are suggesting a solution to addiction beginning with mindfulness. As explained to me, in these programs, mindfulness evolves smoothly into the teachings of the 3 Principles, which is insight-based and forms the heart of the recovery process there. They are integrating the 3 Principles within a broad program that includes meditation, yoga, massage, etc. The program may offer a facility that feels almost resort-like as the ideal environment.

The 12 Steps remind people who are addicted to take recovery "one day at a time," and mindfulness expands this idea into taking life one *moment* at a time. What 12-Step programs tend to suggest is that we are powerless against alcohol and drugs, once they have penetrated our lives. The insight-based 3 Principles teachings allow clients to see that they are not powerless against bad habits such as alcohol and drugs, and that all answers lie in an experience of the Now.

* * *

Personally, I do not mix religion, mindfulness or the 12 Steps with 3P teachings. I simply teach the 3 Principles as uncovered by Sydney Banks. I have found this best, but I do look with interest at other success stories. If a client is religious, I do not hesitate to talk about God. If someone is Indigenous, I do not hesitate to talk about Great Spirit. If one is trained in mindfulness, I do not hesitate to talk about the power of the present moment. I take the same approach with people oriented toward the 12-Step programs—I do not hesitate to talk about ego and higher power. I am interested in expressing the feeling of truth rather than proselytizing about the Principles.

I feel lucky because my core understanding of life revolves around the 3 Principles and personal teachings of Sydney Banks. This has provided me with an anchor or grounding that prevents me from becoming lost in the world's sea of offerings. It is easy to get lost when searching for truth, and it is even easier when applying this search to addiction. I speak from personal experience.

- I see the expression of the 3 Principles, as uncovered by Sydney Banks as forging an understanding with all religions, practices and philosophies. The Principles bring clarity to the spiritual and psychological origins of human behaviour and spiritual destiny. The Principles, by their true nature, will lead to an evolvement of existing offerings.

"All human behaviour and social structures on earth are formed via MIND, CONSCIOUSNESS and THOUGHT."

# Chapter 12

## Summary of Chapters 9-11

You may be curious as to how I integrate my 3P understanding with the status quo approaches in today's world of addiction. I want to emphasize that this struggle was difficult for me to grasp. Initially, I was prejudiced against the 12 Steps, religions and mindfulness.

### POINT 1 — My Credentials

As a young man, I was a hippie pursuing my dreams of unfolding the spiritual reality of life. Like most hippies, I lived outside of society. The youthful hippie movement recognized and rejected society's antiquated and dogmatic ideas. Initially, it did not contribute much to the transformation of the world except as an expression of rebellion and protest.

I've learned, however, that if we desire a positive change in society, we must become part of society. As a natural evolution, the hippie movement petered out, but it is undeniable how many hippies became successful cogs in society and created many of the values of our world. I would say that this is especially relevant for our youth today who have subtly derived healthy values from the initial hippie pursuits. The computer revolution initiated with hippies and evolved into a business model.

My own development shines with what I learned through my hippie exploration. Eventually, though, I cut my hair, got married and had kids. I also started a career and reached a high level of satisfaction in my spiritual and psychological pursuits. This attainment has been sustained by my growing understanding of the 3 Principles.

As I see it, I have only one credential in the world that I can use. This one credential, which supersedes all academic and other professional credentials, is that I am *happy and content*. Because I am happy and content, I can teach happiness and contentment. (For more on this, see coach Molly Gordon's YouTube channel, where I was a guest for her Wholeness Hangout series in the episode titled, "Being Comfortable in Your Own Skin Is Key to Mastery"<https://youtu.be/phNv6G7imD4>).

When my colleague Greg Suchy experienced his spiritual epiphany that allowed him to be free from alcohol addiction, he felt he was living in a vacuum because no one could understand what he was experiencing. Then, he came across the 3 Principles and found a vocabulary to describe it. This not only contributed to how he could share his epiphany with the world, it facilitated his further growth. These factors brought the two of us together to establish the successful Facebook group called "Addiction, Alcoholism & The 3 Principles" with its bimonthly webinar meetings that can also be found as the YouTube series *Addiction, Alcoholism & The 3 Principles.*

The people in the addiction world want to be alive with a happy and content feeling. The way I see it, if what they are following does not take them there, they should look elsewhere!

**POINT 2 — How I View the 3 Principles and Other Psychological Approaches**

The 3 Principles are integrating spiritual understanding back into psychology. We now have "God tools" with which to talk about the healing and doctoring that originates in the spiritual or formless reality of life. Therefore, humankind will evolve into possessing an understanding of a spiritual psychology.

The severe global opiate crisis derives in part from both a lack of understanding in the field of psychology and from its dependency on pharmaceutical drugs. I am not saying that prescription drugs are only negative. They have a purpose, which is to bring a state of peace to an unbalanced, insecure mind. When people become a danger to themselves through attempts at suicide, violence or irrational out-of-control behaviour, drugs can calm down the little mind. However, the need for drugs to continuously maintain this calmness is misguided. There is no need for anyone to be permanently held in a pharmaceutical prison.

Today's powerful drugs are the objects of an addiction, not a solution, and they destroy the lives of many, just as do alcohol and heroin. Not only does the physical body of the user change, so does the user's mind. Users are controlled or influenced by a foreign substance, and anything foreign has visible side effects.

## POINT 3 — The History and Evolution of Psychology

*I want to emphasize, at this point, that some of what I am writing about below comes from listening to ideas initially expressed by Sydney Banks and others. A deeper and clearer appreciation of the topic can be gained from listening to Mr. Banks's videos and audio recordings, and from reading his books. I would recommend the free website www.sydbanks.com as an excellent place to begin your research.*

In the old days, psychology was the study of what we know in the Principles as MIND and CONSCIOUSNESS. Leading psychology professionals decided that they did not know anything about MIND, as this was in the realm of religion. So, it was dropped. Then, they decided that they did not know anything about CONSCIOUSNESS, and the field de-evolved further as they dropped it. Psychology became the study of behaviourism, and this is where humankind became misled.

By definition, psychology is supposed to be the "logic of the psyche," and psyche is a psychological word for "soul." So, psychology in its original form is the scientific study of the "logic of the soul."

As psychology in its present form took hold, society's perspective on mental health became problem-oriented rather than health-oriented. Dr. William Pettit Jr, a long-respected 3P-based psychiatrist, said that when he went to university, he never studied mental health. Because his studies revolved around mental illness, he became an expert in mental illness rather than mental health. And it wasn't until he came to an understanding of the 3 Principles, that he started to help his clients by guiding them to their innate mental health.

This is important because it shows that the study of mental illness is in the process of being replaced by the practice and study of mental health by an increasing number of psychologists and psychiatrists in the world. They will eventually lead the way to a new renaissance in the field of mental health. (see <https://youtu.be/ePgg-R8h6Q0> Dr. Keith Blevens talks about this new paradigm).


## POINT 4 — Are the 3 Principles Going To Replace Religions?

It is ironic is that the 3 Principles represent no threat to existing religions. Let me try to explain this with an example.

A few years ago, I had a talk with the wife of a Jewish rabbi, Chana Rosenblatt, who is also a 3P Practitioner. I asked her how she saw the relationship between Judaism and the 3 Principles. She stated she had no conflict or confusion about the two. She saw the 3 Principles as universal principles that create everything. For her, her choice of expression is in being an Orthodox Jew. She loves her connection to Hashem (a Hebrew word for "God") while living with the understanding that the 3 Principles have brought her. Radiating through her was a sacred feeling about the spirituality of life. She saw that what Judaism points to the same essence as what the 3 Principles do.

Her explanation clarified the scenario for me, and I directly applied her perspective to my understanding of how I could celebrate Native spirituality and the 3 Principles. What is also thought-provoking, regarding the above scenario, is that I am a Jewish man who does not practice his spirituality through Judaism, while she is a Jewish woman who prefers to celebrate her spirituality through Judaism and its teachings of ancient wisdom.

What I see joyfully is that we are both right—she is right for her, and I am right for me—yet we both love our understanding of the 3 Principles and how that understanding has successfully transformed our lives into a greater degree of happiness and contentment.

SECTION 4

IMPORTANT TOPICS

REVOLVING AROUND ADDICTION AND
ALCOHOLISM

# Chapter 13

## Blind Spots, Setbacks and Insights

It is good to note that you and I are never perfect. The challenge with the psychological makeup of human beings is that we all have difficulties seeing our blind spots.

Consider a car. No matter what car we drive, there will always be blind spots. If we are unaware of them, it is quite easy to crash into another car when changing lanes. After an accident or even a near miss, however, we will likely pay much more attention to the blind spots and drive more safely.

A psychological blind spot is when we fool or lie to ourselves, or when we are unware of what is creating our habitual difficulties in life. We become victim to our beliefs and bad habits.

Here's an example from the world of business. In an earlier career, I delivered effective business services to clients. One pipe company had an energetic, charming and youthful president, who was extremely aggressive at landing contracts. But he had a blind spot that would eventually have caused his business to fail. I told him that he should take me out for lunch, and that this was going to be the best lunch he had ever paid for. We went to a fairly expensive restaurant, and after eating and chatting, I took out the statistics on his company.

The accounting showed that his business was booming. Sales were continuing to rise by about 200 percent per year. I asked him how he thought his company was doing. He enthusiastically expressed delight, then he added that the company seemed to always have a cash-flow problem. He explained this was probably due to the increasing volume of sales. I really liked his optimism.

Calmly, I said, "Let me show you something. Every time you sell $1.00 of your product and services, it costs you $1.25." He looked incredulous as I illustrated this on a notepad. After he grasped the full extent of this simple fact, he smiled and said, "Yes, this is the best lunch I have ever paid for."

The next year, when I came to clean up a few other issues in his business, he was smiling and full of gratitude. Sales were down by 50 percent, but profits were now substantial. Not only was his business easier to operate, he was making a sizeable return because he only took on contracts in which he made $$$. The company was no longer short of cash, and he had matured as its leader.

To reiterate, when I showed him the facts, his natural common sense kicked in and he knew how to solve the problem. I have shown many businesspeople facts like this—some see it, some don't.

These days, I sense the presence of Principles—the precious understanding of MIND, THOUGHT and CONSCIOUSNESS, as uncovered by Sydney Banks—but without a heightened awareness of them, I would not grasp how MIND works. Knowing that the Principles are my true nature has much to do with it. My life is filled with stories of how blind spots had kept me a prisoner of my beliefs. When the prison doors opened, I walked into a finer world. I experienced magical and easy events, which enriched my life and allowed me to impact other human beings in a calm, laid-back manner.

Now, let us shift to the topic of helping those in addiction-recovery programs. One major difference between 3P-based addiction programs and many other recovery programs is the approach to clients' blind spots.

I have personally seen recovery programs that innocently demean human beings. As previously mentioned, clients in these programs are often labelled as permanently diseased. People who are addicted are informed that they must continue to work the program for the rest of their lives because their next impulse can send them back down the dark tunnel of addiction. Often, positivity, jokes and seeing the bright side of life are scoffed at as being unrealistic, or as going against the regiment of the program. Counselors, sponsors or people in charge may even snigger at the clients, implying that they are fooling themselves when they share a light-hearted or positive belief about themselves. There can be an insistence that clients see themselves as extreme losers or as being unwise, with the idea that this "realization" or "acceptance" will help them to eventually come out as winners. Participants' natural good mood during these sessions often sinks. (Of course, not all recovery programs are like this, and many do emphasize positivity, self-esteem, comradeship and support.)

Conversely, 3P-based addiction programs teach that we all have innate health and wisdom to which we always have access. These can never be lost, and this is where we go for our healing. Realizing this has allowed people who are addicted to experience their own vulnerability without being victimized by negative feelings. This is especially useful when they encounter setbacks.

When people with addiction experience helplessness—or, as I define it, not being perfect (which is true for everyone)—to then realize that they are innately wise leads to hopeful and empowering feelings. Saying this another way, when people have the experience of not acting on a negative thought or belief, they automatically enter the domain of inner freedom and security. They are more secure because they now understand that the outside circumstances do not control them, and that they are never broken.

It's strange to say, but it seems to me that one purpose of the outside world is to show us that we are only safe inside ourselves. No amount of money, power or status provides the same deep contentment as the feeling of being inside universal CONSCIOUSNESS, because the latter is eternal and spiritual in nature. Money, for instance, is fleeting, merely a human-created concept of a medium of barter and trade. As an object, it has its uses in the realm of form, but that is all. You and I live both in the form and in the formless. The form is physical, while the formless is spiritual.

This is what Sydney Banks came to understand. Up until one point in his life, he had not seen that the three sacred principles of MIND, THOUGHT and CONSCIOUSNESS are the building blocks to all psychological realities we experience here on earth. He'd had an understandable blind spot. Then, in a very few seconds, he no longer had one. It was the same as with Einstein. For much of his life, he had not seen that E=mc², and then, at one point, he did.

And it is the same with people with addiction. They are drowning in a sea of confusion, and then, at some point, they aren't. This happens when we are lucky enough to grasp what MIND is. Many, like Greg Suchy (see Introduction), have had a revelation like this, and in a few seconds, they were no longer addicted to alcohol. Understanding about MIND—the "higher power of life"—gives all human beings a second chance every second of their lives.

And why should this not be true? People come back from the dead. People are miraculously saved from life-ending diseases. People who are pessimistic and filled with complaints at one stage of their lives are not necessarily the same at a later stage. Even world peace is a possibility if the collective consciousness of the world would wake up a little bit more and take a look at their blind spots. Everything and anything is possible.

**Allow your thoughts to soar like the eagles,**
**Turning your dreams into Reality**

To further explore the ideas in this chapter, please visit the YouTube channel *Addiction, Alcoholism & The 3 Principles* and watch the video titled "Blind Spots, Setbacks and Insights."
<https://youtu.be/Cd8COI7QwYU>

# Chapter 14

## Urges Are Powerless

What is it like to be addicted to hard drugs? As one addict explained it to a colleague, "It is like always floating two inches below the surface of water, looking at the light above the water, trying to break the surface in order to inhale a fresh breath of air." The need for air is our desperation to live, and when breaking the surface, the gasp of air is life-saving.

This book would be incomplete if we did not talk about urges or relapses. Urges are one of the most misunderstood psychological phenomena we can experience. They can be felt as all-powerful, creating the illusion that we have lost contact with our free will to think and do whatever we want. Urges come whenever they want, and if acted upon, they can cause great emotional, financial and physical destruction in their path. One generally ends up feeling disappointed, frustrated and hopeless in the wake of this seemingly omnipotent power. Yet, there is an answer, by way of understanding, to dealing with urges.

Here is the key question regarding urges: *"How can we get free from the heavy and oppressive feeling that we are feeling right now?"* We feel like we are in prison, which is actually a mental trap with the illusion of no outlets or escape hatches. It feels like we cannot defend ourselves. We believe in these thoughts, yet we know somehow that they are untruths.

Here is one **clue**. Urges are thoughts that come in waves, and if you are unaware of or do not understand how they work, they will drown you. If the wave catches you, you will succumb almost every time to the convincing "logic" of the little mind. If you see how waves of thoughts work or what a thought actually is, the wave will flow on by and leave you alone. I know this sounds crazy, but when you see how to step aside from the urge, you will walk into a normal world. This world of normalcy feels like heaven because you are "yourself" again without any artificial mindsets dominating and controlling your mental being. You have found the escape hatch to freedom.

These waves are a separate reality. They come and go, especially if we understand what creates them. They are temporary realities, yet we believe them to be permanent. That is the **clue** of separate realities. I am experiencing them in the moment, yet what is causing them to continue to exist is *lack of consciousness*.

Joel Drazner, a resilience coach with several years of training in the Principles, says, "I don't see that there is a personal free will to give up. What you call 'God's free will' (or what I might call 'free will itself') is what all of us, without exception, are a product of. So, no matter what we think, or think about what we think, or how we choose to act upon what we think, or whether we think we should drop a previous thought—all of that is coming from the same Source. And, to me, I think it's important that people know *that*, instead of splitting it into 'God's' vs. 'our' free will."

In my mind, he is correct, but approaching the topic from a different perspective, I would like to examine free will from the point of view of being an ordinary and spiritual being. We come to know that, throughout our lives, all of us have strong negative thoughts from time to time. So, it's not a matter of whether they occur but whether we *understand* the role of THOUGHT when they do occur. If we understand that strong, compelling feelings are only thoughts, at some point we may see the folly of our ways. Or, even better, we may experience an insight about our thinking, or about innate health, which will automatically create a better understanding of being free of the urge.

My co-host on the YouTube addiction series, Greg Suchy, offers another **clue** to urges. He teaches clients to understand that the good feeling of wanting a drink comes from the initial thought that they would like a drink. The drinking of the liquid actually does not create the good feelings. It is when clients make the decision to go to the bar that the good feeling is experienced.

Greg finds that this simple clarification often brings new understanding of how to break the habit, or compelling nature, of addiction. People break the addiction by seeing that they are not at the mercy of their THOUGHT-created-feelings. If people understand where the feeling is coming from—THOUGHT—they will be less of a pushover when experiencing these urges. It is important to psychologically understand that separation of THOUGHT and feeling is not true. Merely seeing this insightfully has liberated many to become free of the addictive urge.

Another way of saying this is that we have the appearance of two thought systems permeating through us. One is the Universal THOUGHT system, and the other is the personal, or ego-based, thought system. The Universal THOUGHT system is where all harmony, good feelings and true freedom exist. This is where our true nature is found and exists before the creation of form; in other words, before the formation of us as a human being.

We also appear to have a human thought system, with its intellectual assistant called the brain. The brain is a biological computer that stores past memories. The primary functions of the brain include relaying information between the brain and the body; supplying some of the cranial nerves to the face and head; and performing critical functions in controlling the heart, breathing and consciousness. The average person has between 50,000-60,000 thoughts per day (many of which are repetitive), and whichever ones we act upon are the ones that we experience in our bodily and emotional reality. Many consider the brain to be the source of our reality and/or our thinking. This is not true, but this misconception assists the ego. We, as human beings, are not separate from MIND, yet ego-thinking insists that we are unconnected.

Here is another **clue**. For all of us, the above description is our problem. We pay attention to ego instead of Universal THOUGHT. So, let's explore how to make ourselves less vulnerable to our unconscious and conscious thoughts and feelings. One of the most powerful ways is to let go of the image or belief that these urges or series of thoughts always have and always will control us. They do, until they don't!

Only wisdom can show us this. The only place we can experience this wisdom is deep within. Surprise, surprise. We have to solve our own puzzles. Surprise, surprise. We are looking everywhere except where the puzzle can be solved. And it is most often found when we are in a balanced, positive or quiet state of mind. Then we may See, that we create our own experience, moment to moment.

The following story from the Indigenous tradition illustrates this last point:

* * *

## Story of the Three Spirits

Alita's 6-year-old niece was sitting on her lap, her big brown eyes eagerly looking into Alita's wise twinkling ones.

The little girl pleaded, "Auntie, please tell me your favorite story."

Alita began:

> This is an old Algonquin story told by a very wise Elder . . .
>
> Many, many years ago there were three Gods, or Spirits, living with the People. The Spirits had to make a big journey, which took them far, far away. This, they were happy about, but they had to leave behind their Special Powers, which were a gift from the Great Spirit. This worried them because the People were not in a good place—they were dissatisfied, selfish and confused.
>
> Then, the First Spirit said, "I know, I know where to leave our Powers. Let us leave them at the top of the highest mountain."

"No," the others said, "the People are so sneaky and scheming; they will find the powers and use them for their own bad purposes." The others agreed.

Then, the Second Spirit said, "I know, I know where to leave our Powers. Let us leave them at the bottom of the deepest ocean."

"No," the others said, "the People are so sneaky and scheming; they will find the powers and use them for their own bad purposes." The others agreed.

Finally, the Third Spirit said, "I know, I know where to leave our Powers. Let us leave them where they will never think to look for them—let us leave them deep inside themselves."

And that is where they left them, where the People would never think to look for them, right below their own noses!

**And that is why all humans are blessed with unlimited potential, an ability to dream, and an abundance of love and self-esteem, if they can SEE.**

\* \* \*

People who are addicted are not powerless when it comes to alcohol and drugs. Urges are thoughts based in fear and insecurity. They create the illusion of being the whole world. It is only in the wrong use of the Principle of THOUGHT that we become victims to urges. We have simply, innocently misunderstood our experience in the moment.

When one sees that there are two apparent thought systems—the Spiritual (Universal THOUGHT), which will always lead us and comes from our True Self, and the personal, which most often leads us in the wrong direction—natural common sense prevails. Life becomes simpler and more peaceful because we allow our personal thoughts to harmonize with the spiritual dimension of life. Wisdom shines through, revealing that life is a spiritual expression via a world of THOUGHT.

"Never forget . . . we live in a world governed by our thoughts and negative thoughts can enter our heads so fast that it is virtually impossible to control them. However, if you can see that they are only thoughts and you refuse to put life into them, they are harmless. If you can do this, you may be surprised by the positive effect it can have on your life."

# Chapter 15

## Relapse

We, as human beings, are mentally, physically, emotionally and spiritually affected by every action, thought and feeling. This is the human experience. The only reason someone experiences a relapse, or repeated relapses, is because there is something very simple that they *do not yet* grasp, an innocent misunderstanding of their experience. This book points to how one can access this understanding, either all at once or a bit at a time.

When one experiences the power of "not knowing," they are saying they are wide open to observing and learning. Understanding relapse would then become like a university course. The open-to-learning person who is addicted will probably end up noticing that the *personal struggle* is the real problem, not the addiction. The struggle may be defined as a battle between two mighty opponents. One opponent is doing everything in its power to maintain a false image that "it knows all the answers" versus the other opponent "who knows that he or she does not know the answer but is open to finding it out."

Greg Suchy, my co-host, says, "There is a deep spiritual meaning to relapse. We human beings are always trying to feel better than we feel right now. Relapse doesn't mean that you have failed. It is part of the human experience; it is part of the desire to reach that part of ourselves where we feel good or OK. If relapse happens, move on. It is giving the energy of attention to relapse that causes more problems because we have guilt, shame and remorse piled on to it. Making yourself guilty is not going to help. If it happens, there is no reason to dwell on it—just move on!"

When Sydney Banks had his enlightenment experience, he turned to his wife and said, "I am home! I made it!" Surprisingly, when wc access wisdom, we come to the same conclusion. Being home is our destiny, our fate and our direction in life.

Yes, when we experience idleness or challenging outside circumstances such as a breakup with a partner or bankruptcy, it becomes difficult to see this clearly. And I agree that it is better not to let an alligator bite your leg off because the personal pain will be excruciating. Yes, it is better to choose to walk around the alligator. This is common sense. Yet, because we are *always home*, I can say with absolute certainty, there are no mistakes. There are just outside experiences that help us see that there is nowhere to go, but instead to just be where we already are. What a paradox!

What is there to be afraid of? Certainly, every feeling we have is our own, and the techniques and strategies we used to manage, cure or resolve them did not work, so let's look in another direction. Here are a few examples.

One client, let's call him John, was very anxious and nervous because he was leaving the comfort of the recovery centre. Compounding this insecurity, he was scared to ever be idle because he thought idleness would take him back to the street and hard drugs. Interestingly, two weeks earlier at this class, John was experiencing a high level of consciousness, expressing perfection in everything he was seeing.

Now he was rattled. He also confessed to having trouble with his girlfriend because she was using, and he believed it would drag him back into that troubled world he hated. It was easy to point John in the direction of quieting his mind and catching a positive feeling. In the end, I told him that if you cannot catch a positive feeling, at least you can share one with whomever comes into your life. This, he knew, for he'd had experience that sharing and having gratitude are pathways away from the addiction.

Another client, let's call him Howard, explained that he had the same girlfriend scenario. He goes to help his girlfriend when he is not using, and she drags him back into the addiction; and vice versa, when she is clean, he drags her back into it. This cycle had been going on for years. Yet, he positively glowed when recounting his best time ever—11 years ago, when his baby girl was born. He loved her so much, and he viewed her arrival as being given a purpose in life. The feeling he was describing was heavenly. I told him that the feeling he felt with his baby girl is the healing answer to all his questions. He smiled and relaxed, realizing that he had the answer within himself. It was there, just waiting for him to uncover the love every human being has inside. In the 3 Principles, we call this "innate health."

"And just beyond that lostness

lies a happy, mentally healthy and wise person

lost in a maze of wrongful thoughts."

Addiction, relapse, and pain are ways we erroneously use the greatest gift ever given to humankind (i.e., free will to think whatever we want). This is real freedom. We freely walked into the relapse and can freely walk out if we experience an insight. Once we wake up a little bit more, we simply won't bother to relapse.

In an interview in the *Vancouver Sun* many years ago, Sydney Banks stated something to the effect: "It's not about analyzing and evaluating what the baggage is; it's about understanding that the baggage is simply thought carried through time."

To further explore the ideas in this chapter, please visit the YouTube channel *Addiction, Alcoholism & The 3 Principles* and watch the video on "Relapse" <https://youtu.be/2pcsaTxJxKw>

# Chapter 16

## Freedom From Suffering

Standing Elk listened attentively as many of the sweat lodge members prayed for relief from their personal suffering and for the suffering of others.

One Indigenous homeless man talked about black spirits coming into his dreams and mind, and he prayed for freedom from these demons. Before this expression, he was screaming for freedom from these demons as the "pourer of the water" used tied cedar boughs to spray water on the hot lava rocks. Standing Elk had laid his hand on this suffering man's arm. This helped calm his mind.

When the homeless man finished speaking, a powerful Indigenous lady spoke. She prayed for release from her addictive urges, even though she had not had an alcoholic drink for several years. This same black spirit had plagued her the night before with all its power and fury. After her sharing, another prayed for the return of health for a friend many miles away.

Now, it was Standing Elk's turn to talk. He began:

> When I hear the prayers of the People in this lodge, when you use the word *prayer*, you are actually asking for more understanding with which to free yourself from your suffering. As we experience a deeper feeling of Spirit, we naturally become one with Spirit. This is where the Mother is waiting for us. She has a big smile on her face, with a glowing heart and boundless love, for we have finally arrived at her doorstep.
>
> She will say, "What took you so long?"
>
> You reply, "I have been busy."

She will say, "Busy with what?"

You reply, "I have been busy thinking about my problems, I have been busy suffering, worrying, analyzing, and judging."

She will say, "And has that helped?"

You reply, "No."

She will say, "So why have you been doing it?"

You reply, "It is what all my teachers and my friends are doing, so I have been copying their ways."

The Mother will then say, "Don't do that! You must only listen to Spirit; this will show you who you really are. The other is a waste of time except to teach you that you are going in the wrong direction. The right direction is simple. You and I must walk together forever in Peace and Harmony. This you can trust!"

You protest, but in the end, you realize she is right—*This is your destiny.*

After the sweat lodge ceremony, Standing Elk went up to the Indigenous lady who had prayed about having trouble with her latent addictive urges. He said, "I can help you with that, if you want. I understand more than most in Indian country. I can show you an understanding that will connect you to the Great Spirit and free you of your urges." She said, "I am listening," but she really wasn't. She wanted the answer in one minute.

Standing Elk suggested they meet for an hour or two over coffee. He felt that one day she may phone him and be ready to end the suffering that was preventing her from joining with the Mother Spirit. Standing Elk knew she would have to give up her beliefs in order to ride the golden chariot to the land of knowledge she aspired to.

During the next two weeks, he thought of this lady several times, as he felt uncomfortable with how he had shared with her the last time. When the "pourer of the water" called another sweat, Standing Elk did not want to go. He did not want to talk to this lady. As the Saturday morning came, he was quite sure that he would not go to the sweat, but he made banana bread with blueberries just in case he did decide to go. He filled the Tonka pipe he carries with the 11 powerful herbs that he uses as a mixture for smoking. Finally, he decided to go. When he arrived, he knew it was the right decision.

Much to his surprise, she was there, waiting for him. He gave her a great big smile. He told her he had some medicine for her, woman's medicine called "bear's weed" from Nevada. He told her it would help her with her emotions. She liked that, saying it was exactly what she needed right now. She was open to the medicine—this was her way.

A sweat generally consists of four rounds. In the fourth round of this sweat, the "pourer of the water," or leader of the sweat, gave her the pail of water with tied cedar boughs in it, which indicated she was to lead the round. She talked openly about her troubles and then said, "The Elder has a story to tell."

Standing Elk told a shortened version of the "Boomerang Story" (see Chapter 2). He sensed that the woman needed to be directed into how CONSCIOUSNESS is the spiritual source of everything, and how her thoughts create her reality. Spirit does the rest. Unfathomable power entered the lodge.

After the final sweat round, Standing Elk and the lady talked for a while. It was a good teaching, just not over coffee as he had imagined it might have been. Instead, it was in a setting she could accept. This is the Indigenous Way.

I hope my readers can see this. You cannot ask an Indigenous person to understand your way of thinking. They have their own way. It is up to us to get some kind of an inkling of the Indigenous way without losing the essence of our own wisdom. After all, if we are truly 3P Practitioners, we should be teaching our clients what they do not understand, but in a way that communicates to and connects with their minds and hearts. Asking them to step inside your bubble is not their way. They already understand and are aware that MIND exists in everything, except they call it Great Spirit, the Great Mystery, Creator or by many other names, such as Wakan Tanka.

By the way, after six months had passed, the homeless Indigenous man's life had miraculously been transformed. He had taken to the ancient Indigenous teachings. He had become an apprentice pipe carrier. He no longer was homeless or reusing, and he had gained weight, looked fantastic, and was in great spirits. A Navaho healer has helped him considerably, along with the "pourer of the water's" spiritual guidance and use of ceremonies.

**Indigenous see Spirit in Everything, whether in form or formless.**

# Chapter 17

## A Serious Topic, But Not a Serious Feeling

It is interesting how many times I have to repeat the words of this title in my 3P addiction classes. Addiction is serious; it is possibly the number one destroyer of life out in the world. However, experiencing a heavy feeling or teaching with heaviness towards this topic is counterproductive.

Let me try to explain it this way. The world loves negativity. For instance, TV news anchors and talk-show hosts frequently conduct their discussions around fear and insecurity. They seem to relish delving into any serious topic of negativity.

It is obvious why the world is like this. Many ordinary humans are mired in ego thoughts of "poor me" or "I know better than you do." Many political leaders do not trust others because they, themselves, are untrustworthy. These heads of state view the world as projections of themselves, rather than leading their constituency in the direction of hope, optimism, peace and wisdom. This lack of compassion and understanding produces disorientation and bewilderment.

When I look at addiction, for the most part, I do not feel pain or suffering. I am not mired in a deep feeling of seriousness. Because I know that is the wrong way! Yet, in many addiction programs, a serious mood is heavily emphasized.

I love working with the heavily addicted. I love to laugh with them; I love to hear their wisdom. I love their smiles of relief when they feel and recognize their innate health and spirit. I love the hope it brings when they see or feel the power of the Principles or want to know more about Sydney Banks and to read his materials.

It is obvious that happy, content teachers or facilitators will bring more joy and fulfillment into the class they are teaching. That sort of outlook will build positive momentum. And no, it will *not* entice the sufferer into relapsing. A tough attitude harms many a sensitive soul. If I was in that kind of serious or heavy-handed program, I would immediately rebel against such an approach. I could not stand having people telling me that I am condemned to a lifetime of suffering, or that I would be mentally diseased for the rest of my life.

Addiction, from my perspective, is a comfortable and uncomplicated subject to teach.

Phase 1 is fundamental. We share something with clients/students that they do not yet understand. But just as all humans do, they crave for a spiritual insight and a positive feeling within themselves. When this is experienced, this opens the pathway toward a cure to addiction.

Phase 2 is an understanding of the role of THOUGHT. Once they have experienced this positive feeling, we help the clients/students to not innocently repeat the old thinking patterns behind their old suffering feelings. Our personal mind performs best when it is flowing and harmonious with Divine MIND. This flowing state of mind allows life to come to us, rather than us trying to be the controller of our reality. It allows us to let go and be unattached to undesirable events in our lives. It produces clarity.

The rest is left up to Spirit. The sufferers will evolve over time to where they can attend to their own healing. They will transform themselves, many times not noticing that Spirit does the actual transformation. Insight will change them forever. *They will do their best and allow the spirit to do the rest.*

I know this sounds over-simplistic. *But that is the key to how it works.* And is it serious? Sorry, it is not. Unless you think it is!

**A VERY INTERESTING story highlighting the above teaching:**

98

My daughter Cari is a Grade 2 teacher. I felt honored when a few years ago she asked me to join her, with the approval of the principal, for one morning a week in her classroom for a school year. Initially, she asked me to come in to work with three difficult students, but I told her I would only come in if I could be with all the students. She agreed. I did not want to draw attention to the ones she identified as having difficulty. That year came and passed, and we enjoyed it so much, I just kept coming in for the following years. During my time there, I would teach to the class of 24 by using stories that had personal meaning to me. In one of my visits, the students gathered in a half circle sitting on the floor. I read a story from *My Guide Inside*—a 3 Principles curriculum book for schoolchildren developed by Christa Campsall and Jane Tucker of 3 Principles Ed Talks. As is my style, I taught them in my own way and based on my own instincts.

One day, I was relating a story from the book of a boy who was bullied. This story was told with two different possibilities. One scenario presented the boy reacting negatively to the bullying, which was accompanied by a lot of stress in his life; and the other had him feeling very secure in the face of the bullying experience. The results in the second scenario were very positive.

After this story, a lightning bolt hit me, and I asked the 8- and 9-year-olds, "What is stress?" To both Cari's and my surprise, none of the students knew what stress was, but they knew their parents had a lot of it.

We looked at each other, almost in shock, as we both realized that, to the kids, stress is not a disease or a problem or even a real thing. It is just something made up, which adults define and label, thus creating all those biochemical reactions in their bodies and minds, and in turn they innocently model and teach this behaviour to their kids.

When I later related this same story about the children's reaction to the recovery centre addiction class I was teaching at that time, one of the clients got quite upset. "But they are still experiencing stress," he asserted. "Yes," I replied, "They are, but they get over it in a relatively short period of time, usually in a few minutes, while you often take two or three weeks to get over something."

His eyes opened wide, and he saw it! The kids process stress the wise way, while many adults process stress unwisely. By being exposed to the teachings of the 3 Principles, he may have seen that his unwise way involved taking the stress too seriously. He may have even seen that this seriousness was created from his thinking, or that he was using the principle of THOUGHT unwisely.

Now that is a consistent challenge for those who are addicted. Much of their problem with addiction is caused by being too serious!

When I began teaching at the recovery centre, I often started the class by saying, "Lighten up." It often seemed at first like I was attending a funeral. They were working hard at being serious. Nothing, and, I repeat, nothing is worse for solving a problem than being overly serious about it. It dominates your mind, your consciousness and your whole being. That seriousness does not allow for innate wisdom to rise to the surface. It keeps you stuck in the heaviness of the situation.

Many cannot seem to get rid of their addiction—they are burnt out trying to get rid of it, much like university students burn out during exam time. They are studying so hard that the human mind gets overtired. Our minds need to relax and empty out.

**Our little mind is a concept maker. In that, it does a great job, except that many of the concepts are illusions created from false gods.**

From Elsie Spittle's book *The Path of Contentment*:

Sydney Banks stated: "Don't trouble yourself worrying about what you have done wrong, Elsie. When you become conscious of your True Self, you will find a whole new world, filled with beauty, understanding and love . . . Stop trying to figure it out, Elsie. Just listen for a feeling, and the understanding will come. You can't find truth with your intellect. You find truth through a feeling, which brings insight."

# Chapter 18

## Recovery From Ego—A Secure Mind

When we are repeatedly complaining and wanting more—more money, more love in a relationship, a better job, etc.—this takes us away from the power of feeling secure. In this state of mind, we lose our gratitude for what life is giving to us in the moment.

Ego is simply your personal thinking while believing you are unconnected to MIND (God). While we can never completely give up ego, we can understand that it holds none of what we are calling the keys to life.

It seems we can say that what Sydney Banks experienced was the death of the ego.

In my opinion, we are looking for recovery not from addiction but from ego. In the minds of professionals in today's society, and what is brainwashed into the minds of those addicted, the only viable and successful result is the elimination of addiction.

A lady from a recovery program I taught stated that she was not interested in only getting rid of her addiction. Wanting more for her life, she asked, "What good would it do me if I wasn't addicted but was still unhappy and still left feeling insecure?"

She understood a key aspect of life. To be healed, to go inside and experience a secure MIND is the solution to all human suffering including from addiction. From that secure place, she will experience happiness and contentment, and eventually forgive and forget her addictive thoughts.

The question of being controlled by addiction evolves or transforms into the query, "Are we controlled by our beliefs?" Once we see what ego is, the next step is to *forget about it completely*. This is often aided by not consistently talking about it. In many addiction programs, they never stop talking about ego, and how to deal with it.

*If I believe in my thoughts and the little mind speaking so confidently to me,*

*what chance do I have to break my addiction?*

*The answer is simple—NONE.*

The problem with being addicted is that we believe the noise in our head. We are playing with dynamite. However, I am suggesting we can temporarily still the noise that ego makes in our little minds, or, at least, head in the direction of this stillness or meditative state of mind.

For me, to use the mind wisely means not polluting it with negative desires. I do this mainly by disregarding much of what my little mind is talking about. Many will say, "Easier said than done," and that is sometimes true. The difficulty with what they are saying is that most people do not understand the relationship of Universal MIND and personal mind.

"An important thing to realize

is that *Universal Mind* and *personal mind*

are *not* two minds thinking differently,

but two ways of using the same mind."

The 3 Principles have changed my life. They have guided me to a powerful and beautiful life, limited only by my lack of understanding. I sense that these Principles exist, and they guide me home whenever I get lost in my thinking.

If I knew better, I wouldn't voluntarily dip into lower moods; but from lower levels of consciousness, I will experience what I need to know and, at the end of this experience lays a great big pot of gold—*this is what I now understand.* This pot of gold easily makes up for whatever struggles I go through.

Intuitively, we, as thinking creatures, understand that ego does not make sense. We love our personal thoughts. In fact, we are often addicted to them. They must be true because we are agreeing with ourselves that they are absolutely the most correct thoughts in the universe. Be careful, you are the fool chasing your own tail.

# Chapter 19

## The End of a Bad Habit and Co-Dependency

I had the privilege of mentoring a group of six in South America for a couple of months. The group was very expressive in their feelings of love, laughter and connection to God, along with a genuine passion for learning more about the 3 Principles. Over that time, the group had found a willing volunteer with an unknown problem in order for me to demonstrate how to share the understanding of the 3 Principles. Initially, I felt apprehensive, as this was the first time I would be teaching a client in front of an audience. Luckily, before the session I experienced an insight: *All mental problems are the result of overthinking. There is only one cause of all problems—overthinking.* I felt at ease. No matter what issue, problem or scenario the client would bring up in its various disguises, I knew the answer. When overthinking calms down, there are no more problems. There is just wisdom.

On first meeting with the client (and the audience), he initially complained about overdrinking. But I saw this as just a symptom, that the overdrinking was not the real issue, so that was disregarded. As we talked, he mentioned "ego." After a few queries I could sense that he did not understand ego. We explored his misunderstanding, and then I told him I had the perfect solution for what was bothering him. He opened his ears wide with a look of anticipation, and I said, "Relax!" After that, every question he asked had the same answer, that a relaxed mind is a happy and content mind.

I was pleased that he returned for another session. This time, before I began helping him, I asked each member of the group what they had seen in the prior session, and to my surprise most had not understood much at all. They could recite their memorized 3P understanding, or what I call the book knowledge of the Principles, but they could not relate their understanding to the client and his personal needs.

After explaining about not trying to fix the client's problems with regurgitated phrases, I began once again with the client. Just as Mette Louise Holland, a Danish 3P psychologist and author, once wrote to me about one of her clients, this was the revelation for this client: "The client comes to realize he is such a beautiful soul, who, like all of us, has to get into a deeper level of consciousness. *This deeper feeling is his true nature, and the ego thinking is not!*"

Later, I described this same story to a troubled mother in North America whose two sons suffered from alcoholism. She asked me if I had ever had an addictive problem. I told her that everyone has bad habits.

I described to her what had seemed the worst bad habit in my past. When I was growing up, my father had a nasty temper. Even though he was one of the kindest and best-liked men in the town in which we grew up, his temper would flare strongly and often. Thus, I thought it was normal to have a temper. My ex-wife and kids hated my bad temper, but I could never see what the problem was. For me, it seemed normal and matter of fact. Whenever I became stressed, I blew up. Once I blew up, I experienced relief and rebounded to a normal non-stressed-out space. I felt great but, alas, everyone else did not.

Then, one day, I was helping out an Indigenous friend out by babysitting her 13-year-old son, who also had a vicious temper. He exploded in typical fashion, and I saw something that changed my life. When he exploded, whatever he was saying was total nonsense. It occurred to me, "I wonder if, when I am angry, it is the same with me—what if what I am saying is also total nonsense?"

Until that moment, I had always assumed that everything I said while angry was totally correct. My little mind had always convinced me that I was right. But what if I had been fooling myself? And then I saw it very clearly—*I was*! As hard as this may be to believe, at that moment, I lost 95 percent of my temper. Without any effort, I had been transformed.

My kids have really appreciated this, and so has my ex-wife. It has changed my relationships, especially with my children. In fact, it has been so long that I can hardly remember the other Harry. Of course, occasionally, when I am overtired, I may briefly lose my temper.

So that was my bad habit; I had been looking for relief. It was how I dealt with my imbalances and stress. The intention behind that behaviour is the same as for those with alcohol and drug addiction. The drinker feels disconnected and, repeatedly, takes a drink or a drug in order to feel better. This becomes a pattern and a habit over time.

So, the mother asked, what is it that breaks this pattern? I told her of a story that I always found fascinating. While at a 3 Principles training centre, I met a woman who had been a cocaine addict for 25 years. She had achieved the miracle of becoming totally free of the addiction. I asked her how it happened. She said, "When I found a feeling better than the cocaine, that is where I went."

She turned to cocaine whenever her nerves were tense, her head aching, and her heart sad and depressed. However, the Principles pointed her towards her spiritual essence. Connecting is the best feeling in the world. The other, addiction to a substance or activity is neat, but empty and temporary compared to the alive feeling of life. That is the case with all addiction, and it is the reason that whenever I am teaching to those struggling with addiction, I am looking for a feeling of hope! That is a step in the right direction.

The mother ended our conversation by telling how the 3P understanding had helped her to feel love and compassion for her sons while not feeling guilty or responsible for what they were doing. Initially, she had to work through the pain of seeing her sons suffer, but now, she feels a healthy detachment to their suffering. She realized that she is not to blame and that what they are going through is what they need for their lives. She has learned not to give up her happiness because of what her sons are going through. And she has learned to access her good feelings and wisdom, which makes her a better helper and support for her sons when they reach out to her.

I want to emphasize that we all have bad habits, whether it is overeating, violence, lust, greed, "workaholism," overusing our cellphones or the internet, or binge-watching TV. The cause of all bad habits is overthinking. So, I am suggesting that you relax and enjoy the moment. Give it a try, and while you are enjoying the moment, it would not hurt for you to share a positive feeling with yourself, such as having gratitude for what life is giving you now.

# Chapter 20

# Peace of Mind

No matter what we have experienced yesterday, peace of mind is available today to everyone, including you. Peace of mind is not a concept or a better idea of how to live; it is a reality within. The only time we can effectively talk about peace of mind is when it comes alive in the present moment. It is a feeling that speaks louder than volumes of words; and because it is real, it speaks to and from our hearts and minds. Surprise of surprises, we must feel it alive in ourselves.

The feeling of true peace of mind is an affirmation that we live in a heavenly state here on earth. It allows all humans, no matter what happened yesterday, to live with MIND right now. While this may sound like doctrine, it is not. It is simple common sense. This feeling comes into our awareness because it is us.

"Let your negative thoughts go.

They are nothing more than *passing thoughts*.

You are then on your way to finding the *peace of mind* you seek,

Having healthier feelings for yourself and for others."

I love to say, "You talk *from* Spirit rather than *about* Spirit." Peace of mind and contentment emanate from MIND, and they automatically bring with them gratitude and spiritual sustenance.

How does this apply to the world of addiction? The peace of mind we've been talking about is the healing balm we all are searching for, whether addicted or non-addicted.

At higher levels of consciousness, we feel more connected to True Self or MIND. Knowledge and clarity pours in, allowing us to see how to make our lives that more positive. This is inspirational. How can we deny such power? We can't! When we are living in this profoundly peaceful state of mind, we forget about the reality of addiction. Three weeks or a month pass by, and we realize we have not thought about it. Worrisome thoughts would interfere with the sacredness of the moment, so naturally we move on.

At lower levels of consciousness, peace of mind is still there, but our conscious mind is not aware of it as much. We feel more abandoned or separated from MIND, yet we are working towards what I call the inevitable breakthrough. When we break through, sometimes we will attempt to fight it or ward it off, but the positive feeling is too delightful. Our dreams are being answered. This is undeniable. Who wouldn't want to live in this world? The irony is, we already are!

When, after we have experienced "going inside," from time to time, we drop into a lower level of consciousness, we will recognize that we are doing so. We will become the observer, and at the end of the experience we will uncover a pot of gold. The gold is a new insight, "I did not know something before, and now I do." It is time to enjoy all the gold that life has been throwing in our direction.

Spiritual peace of mind is everyone's answer to addiction. Addiction is simply a manifestation of a lower level of consciousness. It is a game that could not be played without your consent, and every time you experience a lower level of consciousness, it makes total sense to your mind that you should play this game.

One day, you will prefer peace of mind more than playing the game. You won't arrive at this realization through mental effort—not through willpower—but through insight and common sense. We must be honest. We must experience the truth inside. Everything else becomes boring gobbledygook.

Peace of mind can only be an inside-out experience. It cannot come from a book, or another person—it comes from you and *is* you. You are peace of mind.

My advice is to keep looking in the direction of love and understanding. As these become more apparent, we will naturally give up the search. Our job here on earth becomes:

1) Find out who and what we really are

2) Give up the search

3) Do nothing

\* \* \*

At the 2018 3PUK Conference in London, with some 900 attendees, various presenters spoke from their hearts and 3P understanding on all sorts of topics, ranging from living with cancer to experiencing trauma around their kids. They expressed how the Principles assisted them in realizing peace of mind through understanding how we live in the human experience. They were articulate, precise and filled with love. Watching the various presentations and discussions, it struck me that I saw the 3P understanding slightly differently, which is consistent with the fact that we all see truth from different perspectives.

When a man from the audience asked about a personal problem, two caring and wise presenters shared their understanding of the psychological connection to the human experience. As they addressed this man's question, it looked clear to me that everything in life is a perfect design by God. In fact, at that time I was sick with the flu. And while, of course, I preferred not to be ill, I also knew that this sickness was perfection in motion. Aside from various physical discomforts, I had no thoughts of distress. I was peaceful with the sickness because it seemed just what I needed to fully experience the conference in a rich and rewarding manner.

It is in the "doing nothing" that the world is magical. I know it sounds odd, but the "doing nothing" idea I am expressing here is from an inside-out perspective. From this perspective, life is so easy and relaxing, and peace of mind is felt. We all have a second chance, every moment of our lives, if we can see it.

# Chapter 21

## CONSCIOUSNESS—The Perfect Design Master

The only reason we fall into bad habits or negative thought patterns is lack of CONSCIOUSNESS. MIND has arranged itself so that it self-corrects in any moment needed. The joy is that this system is infallible if we are aware that we are Spirit, MIND, God, and are perfectly designed.

As we unveil levels of consciousness, we see clearer and more precisely who and what we are. This will uncover the secret and freedom from the addiction. Remember, at the lower levels of our existence, it appears that outside circumstances control us. Our past controls us when we believe that these outside circumstances or past feelings are real or beyond our innate ability to rise above them.

Once, I was talking to a medical doctor who had a poor understanding of the effect of outside circumstances and actions. I mentioned that we are not a victim of our outside circumstances, and he disagreed. He said, "What about being stuck in traffic?" I said, "Well, while we cannot control the traffic, we can turn the radio on, calm down our negative thinking and have a relaxing time waiting for the traffic to clear up. In fact, we can even be on holiday (mentally) taking the time to let all the thoughts of the day evaporate into thin air."

He acknowledged that this was true, but I could see he never really understood it. It became clear to me that, for him, whenever he got stuck in traffic, he had no choice but to innocently experience anxiety and stress. Don't you see? It is all his thoughts. If he dropped the thought, or relaxed his mind, the situation would seem totally different to him psychologically.

Let me share another example. An Indigenous woman, who had read a draft of this book, loved Chapter 3, "The Victim Story." But she said that I had left out something very important. While she agreed with what was expressed in the chapter, she said I needed to take into account when outside circumstances are the cause of victimhood, such as if one is attacked physically by someone who is mentally dysfunctional or physically stronger. I said, "I am approaching everything from a psychological perspective. While it is true that some outside circumstances/events may be out of her control, how she handles the scenario is totally within her control. If she is aware, she will, as calmly as possible, handle the situation. If she freaks out and feels powerless over the situation, she gives power to her antagonistic attacker.

Now, let's relate these antagonistic attacker thoughts and freaking out to addiction. We have beliefs. Let us say that one of our beliefs is that addiction or alcoholism is a disease. If, in fact, this is not true, the belief will create a whole world of thinking based around this falseness. In this instance, it would be very difficult to understand that addiction is actually a bad habit caused by our negative thinking over a period of time

*I think, and I create!*

*I don't act on a thought, and I create!*

Many will say that the power of addiction is not only mental but physical, and I acknowledge that truth. Luckily, the power of truth is more powerful than any other force in life, including our beliefs around addition. Yet, interestingly, many who are addicted uncover what they need from a huge variety of approaches. And that is perfect as well! I cannot change the world, but I can accept "what is."

# Chapter 22

## Combining the Human Condition With the Principles

For years, I struggled with the meaning of the phrase *the human condition*. Many others have struggled with the meaning of *the spiritual condition*. With these two combined, we have concepts of creation—i.e., the mystery of the universe and our relationship with it.

What we experience as human beings is what I am referring to as the "human condition." The quality of our human condition directly relates to the quality of our thinking and to how we understand silence. Humans have the appearance of living in houses, but actually, we live in our heads, where we create our own separate realities and belief systems

A relative, who lives in Vancouver, traveled to Winnipeg (both in Canada) for my mother's 95th birthday. The relative was disconcerted, feeling it was like visiting a foreign country. Not only was the culture of the city different than her own, but she was having difficulty with the individual cultures of those who attended the birthday celebration. Third, and most important, she concluded that other human beings often have independent ideas along with different attitudes to life.

This is the basis of why most family members do not get along. Each person lives in their head and has no interest in what the other member is thinking. There may even be prejudice against one or two members of the family. The family really loves each other, but their thoughts have created an illusion of opinions, prejudices, disappointments and dislikes. The joke is that most of it is not true but simply each member's own perceived reality.

Humans in low moods often express themselves in less than positive ways. Sometimes, they do so in the most vulgar and insulting manners. They become so upset that whatever they express sounds immature, childish, rather than reasonable and logical.

This occurred for me, too. The insinuations and observations were disappointing, but mostly I felt compassion for the other's heavy feelings since they had difficulty when their point of view was questioned by others.

So, what I have described above is one aspect of the human condition. Without my understanding of the Principles, I could have become lost in the quagmire and quicksand of the reality created by that uncompromising person.

This scenario seemed to ignite a web of bad luck. I had difficulty in Winnipeg with the rental car's baby-seat installation, problems with my Airbnb rental, and then my elderly Mom pooped on the seat of one of the relative's cars. These scenarios were compounded with conflicting ideas expressed by friends and relatives. As I weeded my way through this trip, I found a settling influence. I had been rattled, I had been upset, yet I flowed with all of this in my head and dealt with it as quietly as I could.

The last night with the family, including the frustrated relative, ended up being one of the nicest evenings I had ever experienced. None of us wanted ugly feelings among one another. Without saying a word about the difficult scenarios, we had a fabulous night. The relative and I gave each other a big, loving hug. In the end, the trip had become enjoyable, and as I rolled on home, I had a very comfortable feeling of gratitude for my family. I had loved sharing my Mom's 95th birthday with my family from Winnipeg and Vancouver. The feeling of gratitude multiplied when my mother passed away a few weeks afterwards.

"A family is a place where minds come in contact with one another. If these minds love one another, the home will be as beautiful as a flower garden. But if these minds get out of harmony with one another, it is like a storm that plays havoc with the garden." ~*Buddha*

From my viewpoint, all that we are as human beings is created by God, Spirit or MIND (all three being the same thing)—that which some call the Universal Energy or Intelligence of All Things. We share ideas and feelings via THOUGHT, the creative force of the universe. In the simplest of words, as we evolve into greater levels of consciousness, we become finer human beings, and that is the idea. As we become better-quality human beings, our human condition becomes gentler, easier and more rewarding. Gratitude dominates!

I see life as a circle or a spiral. What goes around comes around. MIND goes around and is inside the spiral. At the very core of its existence, WE ARE. You are the centre of your universe. I am the centre of my universe. This is what I believe Sydney Banks expressed in his talk titled "The Great Spirit," when he was describing his enlightenment experience. He said, "Many years ago, I had the privilege of stepping inside this centre."

In his early teachings, Sydney Banks talked about "what MIND is" as the answer to eliminate all suffering. When the psychologists first discovered his teachings, I felt that he expanded his talk to be about "what MIND is and how it applies to this world." In my opinion, this addition is the human condition.

*What does it mean to be human?*

*What are the basic needs and desires of the human being?*

*What is unique and special about the human existence?*

"There are two basic motivating forces: fear and love. When we are afraid, we pull back from life. When we are in love, we open to all that life has to offer with passion, excitement, and acceptance. We need to learn to love ourselves first, in all our glory and our imperfections. If we cannot love ourselves, we cannot fully open to our ability to love others or our potential to create. Evolution and all hopes for a better world rest in the fearlessness and open-hearted vision of people who embrace life." ~*John Lennon*

"You must not lose faith in humanity. Humanity is an ocean; if a few drops of the ocean are dirty, the ocean does not become dirty." ~ *Mahatma Gandhi*

"If we have no peace, it is because we have forgotten that we belong to each other." ~ *Mother Teresa*

"Only a life lived in the service to others is worth living." ~ *Albert Einstein*

*Buddha Quotes:*

"All that we are is the result of what we have thought. The mind is everything. What we think, we become."

"Hate is not conquered by hate. Hate is conquered by love. This is a law eternal."

"Good men and bad men differ radically. Bad men never appreciate kindness shown them, but wise men appreciate and are grateful. Wise men try to express their appreciation and gratitude by some return of kindness, not only to their benefactor, but to everyone else."

And from *Sydney Banks*:

"All human behaviour and social structures on earth are formed via MIND, CONSCIOUSNESS and THOUGHT."

# Chapter 23

## The Right Use of the Principles

I met an old friend at a car show where 300-400 antique and cool older cars were on display. My friend had an old car in the show, and when I saw him, he looked like he was in heaven. He mentioned that most Sundays he goes to car shows and loves walking around, feeling totally relaxed while being enthralled by the atmosphere, cars and enthusiastic crowds.

When we met for coffee afterwards, I said to him that this is the right use of the Principles. One does not need to know about the concepts of MIND, THOUGHT or CONSCIOUSNESS or even know they are Principles. Since they are our true nature, we use them intuitively and naturally. That is the state of consciousness we primarily want to live in—it is our birthright. This is the state he was living in when he was at the car show.

I told him, "We have to let our mind flow to where all healing exists and where we are one with the Spirit or our True Self. This flow is like being in a river. Upstream there is a bear that poops in the water, and, often, we take a bucket and scoop up the poop as it floats downstream. We then show this poop to everyone, and many opinions of disgust are expressed around it. Then we dump the poop out of the bucket, and before we know it, we scoop up another turd and show it to everyone. The focus is on the poop. We need to see the flow of the river and the beauty of life, rather than working hard at scooping the poop into our bucket."

This is how the Principles work. We don't know or understand all the features, aspects and source of our problems. All we know is that when we go to where they *are not*, we have smooth sailing, no holes in our boat, and we are safe. Feeling safe is the object of the game.

I have learnt much about this from my deceased mother. When she felt safe, she was in the most relaxed, content state of mind possible. She just enjoyed being alive, driving in the car, being pushed around in her wheelchair and hanging out with life. When she felt unsafe, her eyes bulged out and her body tensed. The moment I touched her arm, she immediately returned to a beautiful state of mind—she felt safe once again. Isn't that what you want?

Getting in touch with the 3 Principles guides me back to safety. When I am confused or bewildered by life and its infinite possibilities—good or bad—I check in on my feeling. They are my true guide. If, to my mind, something is happening that seems impossible to grasp or figure out, I check in with my guide. They tell me immediately how things will turn out. Many times, I experience a calm, comfortable and safe feeling. I know I can trust that feeling. And it works 100 percent of the time. These feelings are designed to guide me away from the pitfalls of my intellectual thinking. They take me into Spirit. They take me into truth. They take me into my wisdom.

I feel safe most of the time, and you can feel safe most of the time, because that is everyone's natural state of consciousness. Life becomes so simple, so easy. Life gives so much, because that is the perfect design of life—if we don't interfere by worrying about where the poop is.

At a week-end conference in Stockholm, Sweden, I was teaching about "What MIND Is" and suddenly, I realized: *MIND is silence.* When we step into the silence, we heal. It is that simple.

*Living in fear, in a pessimistic state of mind or*

*worrying about the past or future*

*is the poop.*

*Move gently around these turds, and*

*maybe it is a good idea to leave the bucket at home.*

# Chapter 24

## Summary of Chapters 13–23

Joe Bailey, a 3P Practitioner, stated on the *Addiction, Alcoholism & The 3 Principles* webinar series that there is a common denominator of insecurity that is the basis of all addictions. What this statement implies is that the 3 Principles unify all the various fields of addiction. So, whether one is addicted to drugs, alcohol, sex, gambling, overworking, etc., the science behind the healing of those addictions has been uncovered by Sydney Banks. Joe said, "Mr. Banks explained how life works from the inside out, that we are living in a world of THOUGHT and that all we are feeling in the moment is our thinking in that moment. We are already designed perfectly." In my opinion, when one sees the aforementioned via insight, the road to healing becomes hopeful, it points one in the direction of truth.

Once this happens, gratitude is omnipresent. Life ceases to be full of torture. It becomes easier not to focus on or overthink all the difficult times. It becomes easier to walk into the silence our insight made available to us. Life slows down in our head, and we come to understand that all we have to do is turn to our inner wisdom, be happy and share this happy feeling with others.

Then, the world of the addicted transforms into the world of "happiness and contentment." Sydney Banks stated that "Purity of THOUGHT is the (ladder) to success." And he defined *success* as "happiness and contentment." That is my mantra for my life. Sometimes I seem to forget the mantra, as I am a human being with a thought system that can get troubled and confused. However, the journey is both mysterious and fulfilling.

I do not actually know what the future will bring. I simply know I will enjoy most of it, and, at the same time, drop some more of my bad habits and personal judgments. I suppose that is CONSCIOUSNESS.

# SECTION 5

# HOW DOES IT ALL FIT TOGETHER?

# Chapter 25

## The Starting Point in Your Understanding About Addiction

I watched this perceptive 2015 TED talk by Johann Hari, titled "Everything You Think You Know About Addiction Is Wrong." Mr. Hari, the author of *Chasing the Scream: The First and Last Days of the War on Drugs*, starts out by saying, "It's a century since we made this really fateful decision [in North America and Britain] to take addicts and punish them and make them suffer because we believed it would deter them, it would give them an incentive to stop." Obviously, he is suggesting that this approach does not work, and that it is barbaric, (and I would agree).

Continuing on this theme, he expressed that ". . . there were loads of incredibly basic questions I just didn't know the answer to, like what really causes addiction? Why do we carry on with this approach that doesn't seem to be working, and is there a better way out there that we could be trying instead?" These are fundamental questions for unraveling the mystery of addiction.

Then he introduced a thought experiment, as Einstein might use, in which a section of the audience was asked to imagine they were taking heroin three times a day for 20 days. "We think because there are chemical hooks in heroin, as you took it for a while, your body would become dependent on these hooks, and you would start to physically need them and at the end of those 20 days, you all would be heroin addicts." He felt there was something not right about this story. He gave the example of someone who had broken a hip, was taken to the hospital and given pure heroin for a quite a period of time, and yet that person would not necessarily become an addict.

Still, Mr. Hari admitted that he had believed in the chemical-hooks theories until he had evolved somewhat in his understanding about addiction. Assisting him in this was his meeting with Bruce Alexander, a professor of psychology in Vancouver, B.C., who carried out an experiment that contradicted earlier apparent scientific findings on the subject. In the early 20th century, the chemical-dependency theory of drug addiction derived partly from this series of experiments. As Mr. Hari explains:

> You get a rat and put it in a cage, and you give it two water bottles: One is just water, and the other is water laced with either heroin or cocaine. If you do that, the rat will almost always prefer the drug water and will almost always kill itself quite quickly . . . In the '70s, Professor Alexander comes along and looks at this experiment, and he noticed something . . . We are putting a rat in an empty cage. It's got nothing to do except use these drugs . . . So, Professor Alexander built a cage that he called 'Rat Park,' which is basically heaven for rats. They've got loads of cheese. They've got loads of colored balls. They've got loads of tunnels. Crucially, they've got loads of friends, they can have loads of sex. And they've got both the water bottles, the normal water and the drugged water. But here's the fascinating thing. In Rat Park, they don't like the drugged water. They almost never use it. None of them ever use it compulsively. None of them ever overdose. You go from almost 100 percent overdose when they are isolated to zero percent overdose when they have *happy and connected* lives.

Then, Mr. Hari demonstrates that it is the same for human beings, referring to the example of wounded Vietnam war veterans as an illustration. Many of the wounded were medicated for long periods of time in Vietnamese hospitals with the purest of heroin (much more powerful than heroin purchased on the street), and yet when they returned from active duty to the United States, most did not come back as addicts. They simply returned to their normal lives.

According to Mr. Hari, "Professor Alexander began to think there might be a different story about addiction. He said, 'What if addiction isn't about your chemical hooks?'" The professor then wondered if addiction is about other factors, such as "the cage" or our perception of life and environment.

Mr. Hari then spoke of another professor, Peter Cohen in the Netherlands, who said, "'Human beings have a natural and innate need to bond. And when *we are happy and healthy*, we bond and connect with each other. But if you can't do that because you're traumatized, or isolated, or beaten down by life, you will bond with something that will give you some sense of *relief*. That might be gambling, that might be pornography, that might be cocaine . . . but you will bond and connect with something because that is our nature, that is what we want as human beings."

As you can see, the world of addiction is thought-provoking and requires insightfulness to unravel its deep and dark secrets. The human factor cannot be ignored.

I know for a fact that much of what the world thinks about addiction is wrong. I also think that there is much to unravel in this mystery of solving the opiate crisis, and I would even be bold enough to say that the world of the 3 Principles has only just begun its journey into this investigation.

It is the same for Mr. Hari. He has only begun his investigation, but he is asking some of the right questions. Coming back to his personal questions of unknown answers, "What really causes addiction? Why do we carry on with this approach that doesn't seem to be working, and is there a better way out there that we could be trying instead?" The last section of this book should provide you with some clues or answers to the above questions.

You can draw your own conclusions about all this, but I believe that *stepping into the world of happiness and contentment is the cure to addiction.* Or, at least it's the right place to begin out journey to solving our misunderstanding about addiction. The world needs to evolve into offering a better way to help all those needy and suffering human beings. They are demanding it. They really, really, really would like to leave this behind them.

Can't you hear their cries for help,

YET ALL YOU CAN SAY is,

"It's your fault,"

or

"Wow, addiction seems to be affecting almost every family in North America."

\* \* \*

Debi Muccillo, a 3 Principles colleague and a mother, emailed me to say: "My boys will both be here for our Christmas celebration. My whole litter will be here for the first time in quite a while. Very special blessed time. Big hugs!"

Both of her boys were heavily into alcohol, one going to prison and the other nearly dying several times in the hospital emergency room. Yet, her family was now together in a bountiful way for Christmas. And the biggest miracle of all is that she helped them by finding happiness and contentment within her own consciousness. Then she spread this feeling of love and understanding outward to her boys.

When Debi showed the cover of this book to one of her sons, Adam Clark, he said in reference to his insight, "There were many times in my life that I was walking down the track, and I heard the train coming, and I didn't get off the path."

Ms. Muccillo acknowledges the in-depth mentoring, coaching and counseling into the spiritual nature of the Principles she received from us working together, along with other trainings from other 3P coaches. Yet, it was she and her understanding that made the difference. She heard her sons' cries for help, and she HELPED! Worrying and feeling guilty were of no use. In her case, the spiritual and psychological direction of the 3 Principles led her to the answers she needed to help. In your case, you will find what you need within your own direction or path. But, since you are reading this book, I encourage you take a good and healthy look at the possibility of the 3 Principles providing the sustenance you are seeking.

Isn't that what you want—to uncover the truth about addiction?

**The starting point is simple.**

**You don't know, and stop creating a story that you do.**

# Chapter 26

## The Silence of MIND

Andrea Bocelli is an Italian singer, songwriter, and record producer. He was born with poor eyesight and, following a football accident at age 12, became completely blind. Bocelli has recorded 15 solo studio albums of both pop and classical music, three greatest-hits albums, and nine complete operas, selling over 80 million records worldwide. He has had success as a crossover performer, bringing classical music to the top of international pop charts.

A movie about Andrea Bocelli's life, *The Music of Silence*, depicts him having a very wise teacher from Spain, who taught him more than how to attain perfection in his voice. At the beginning of his work with Andrea, his teacher says, "Silence is the most important and the most difficult."

After Mr. Bocelli's voice matures, the teacher says, "Singers before a performance must remain in a condition of the most absolute *silence*. It is difficult to achieve, and when you have learned how not to need words, you will sense the sound of your own breath, the movement of your own muscles, and the movement of a single strand of hair ruffled on your head. The musical silence will be your guide into the interior of yourself, and that which you discover, you will express through the beautiful perfection of song."

I had the privilege of experiencing just such silence in 1977 on Salt Spring Island at age 28. My then-wife and I had come to live on Salt Spring in order to find the spiritual answers to life via the enlightened teachings of Sydney Banks. We had moved into a little rented trailer on a five-acre, several-million-dollar property overlooking the ocean. As idyllic as the setting was, my wife and I were not happy. While others on the island seemed to live in peace and harmony with their partners and with themselves, we still fought. And we seemed not to grow in wisdom as were many of the others who were listening to Sydney Banks. One day, we attended one of his many gatherings at his home, and we waited until everyone had left. We dragged our weary bodies and minds to Syd, telling him that we had not achieved the happiness that we'd wanted. Tears of sadness were rolling down our eyes. He looked at my wife compassionately and said, "Don't worry, dearie, you will." We left with these encouraging words.

About a week later, I was walking by myself around St. Mary's Lake on the island, in my usual state of mind, tossing and turning with many thoughts, when all of a sudden, all thought stopped! I had mystically stepped into a different world, into a world of silence. True, I was still here on this physical plane, yet not of body. I could hear every sound of the birds chirping, the trees rustling in the wind, and all the colors were luminous. It was as if I was watching all of life around me, not with my eyes, but as God. My mind was all that I was aware of. I had dissolved into CONSCIOUSNESS. There were no moments, just the silence of seeing life in all its splendor and glory. I was One with the universe, and alive with "who I am." It lasted for around three to four minutes, and then I came back to this plane of existence. Thought re-entered my mind, and I was back in my body being Harry Derbitsky.

This silence was golden. After this experience, I never again doubted that the world was spiritual. This sense became the guiding light of my life. Interestingly, even though I would succumb to doubtful and misguided thoughts many times thereafter, the feeling of this experience has always guided and saved me. When I turned 69, after many wonderful lessons from life, I realized more of the essence of this visionary experience. And I understood what had taken so long.


**Life was spiritual, and I knew it!**

# Chapter 27

# I Have a Mind!

I have had the privilege of playing chess with my 8-year-old nephew, Yosef, from Israel. He is brilliant for his age, and I love mentoring and playing with him, via the modern enterprise of internet video communications. Once in a while, when he makes a move, I say to him, "That is not such a good move." He sometimes replies, "I HAVE A MIND!" He is correct. He not only has the right to move wherever he wants, he also has his own thoughts and they are clever, sneaky and wonderful.

He has learned at a very early stage what many adults never learn. He is a clever thinker, and he can brainstorm and figure things out. He even sees brilliant moves in his mind. He visualizes! He deduces! His mind is clear! His mind is creative and precise!

This 8-year-old chess master understands something very important. His mind and God's MIND are One. He is not afraid to tap into the unknown. He is secure in his ability to use the Power of God (Hashem, to him). The reader might call this intuitive or instinctual, but I call it "using his God-given talent wisely," or what Sydney Banks calls, "the right use of MIND."

When he loses, he is excited to play again, to try again, and he really enjoys the pursuit of excellence. He loves to try to out-think me, and even better, he loves difficult positions where there are numerous possibilities. To understand what I am saying, you would have to accept the fact that the best fun is when we are not sure who will win—maybe him and maybe me. It is not the winning that is exciting; it is the "thinking." That is the right use of MIND. He will brainstorm his way through life, enjoying the winning and losing, enjoying life's challenges, and relishing the victory of solving an impossible problem or scenario.

The right use of MIND is for us to understand what MIND is, and then we will know how to use it wisely. Let me give you an example:

You are caught up in your little thinking. You are worried, insecure and fearful. Nothing makes sense, and your self-esteem is low. Your mood is low. You feel hopelessly lost. This "poor me" is what I am referring to as the wrong use of MIND.

You step back from all this negative thinking and relax. You take a bike ride to the ocean and let your thoughts drift wherever—positive or negative, it does not matter. As these thoughts drift, you suddenly notice how beautiful everything is. Mother Earth, via the trees, sky and ocean, is healing you. The energy of the Mother Spirit is connecting you to your True Self. You enter a zone where you are your True Self. You are the Mother! You are the Father! You are One! This is the feeling of MIND.

How powerful is MIND!

This is what Yosef understands. He cannot say it in words, he just knows! He does not have to verbalize what is obvious,

If you have a nose, do you have to know everything about it? No. You just breathe through it. Only when it is broken or bloody do you even notice it. Then it hurts, and the appreciation of a perfectly designed nose comes into play.

This is the perfection of MIND. It gives us a perfect nose, and when it is bloody, it heals itself, sometimes with our help. The reader may say that cancer kills. This is true on the physical level, but on the spiritual level, it heals. This is the perfect result for this human being. We all know one thing—we will die, and our bodies will dissolve into nothingness. Some of us just live longer than others. My mother lived to 95, my father to 80, my uncle to 50—perfect for each of them.

Now, let's take a look at the power behind the concept of MIND.

# Chapter 28

## It's All in the Feeling!

I woke up with a strange feeling. I was extremely uncomfortable. As the day progressed, this negative feeling grew and grew. I was increasingly restless and oh so tired. I tried to rest by going to bed. My mind would not rest. I tried watching TV. I went to the fridge continually to eat snacks, even though my stomach was full. I was so uncomfortable.

Suddenly, amidst the worst feeling possible, I realized that I needed to talk to a colleague who was uploading an important video for me. As I was contacting him via email, because he lives in Europe, I surprisingly felt relief. I was reclaiming something.

My European colleague let me know it was not going well at all. He could not upload the video. He was frustrated, and since the time difference between us was eight hours, he was going to bed. Had I still been experiencing a heavy feeling, his frustration would have drowned me into a sea of despair.

Just like in the world of addiction, when natural good feelings appear, the need for outside stimuli evaporates. Previously, I was not recognizing what the feeling was trying to tell me. All I was doing was personalizing the feeling with more and more thought, and the death spiral magnified. I was identifying with this heavy feeling, which totally clouded my perspective.

Now, it was different. I had a new signal. A fresh idea popped into my head. I could try uploading the video onto my YouTube channel, and then link it to his. An hour and half later, I was announcing to the world about "Greenland & The Mystical Nature of the Principles," with sharing's by eight wise Inuit women, Danish 3P psychologist Mette Louise Holland, and Harry Derbitsky.

- Everything becomes easy after we regain our equilibrium. The bad feeling is a signal. Once I recognized this, the situation quickly resolved itself. It was as if I was doing nothing, but I was waiting for a feeling that would guide me home.

*What does this teach us about addiction?*

Listen carefully. When the positive feeling announces itself, you have to be able to recognize and then follow it. This is especially true when you have problems with relapsing into your addictive pattern. When your level of consciousness rises and you wake up with a good feeling, but your little mind presents you with an "urge," following the positive feeling will set you free. Isn't that simple? Yet sometimes we still turn our back on it.

If you do not follow the positive feeling and instead listen to your persuasive personal thoughts, you will eventually wake up to the fact that the positive feeling was not only a signal but a direction of going home. The little mind is just a noisy, clunky robot saying, "I lie, I lie." Habit is simply us following the robot. Spiritual or positive feelings are from MIND.

There is a saying, "You can't mix oil and water." It is the same with feelings. Here lies the potential answer to all of life's questions— feelings will not only tell you when they are impure, they will also tell you when they are pure,

- Here is the **rule**: If you do not follow positive feelings, then you do not get the benefits of positive feelings.

Let me try to describe what purity of feelings is not.

Sometimes, I feel the magic of my life. Everything seems to be working out, and I feel tremendous gratitude. This is pure. Then, I start to associate my feelings with the amazing results or events that have happened. The second construct is not as pure and always leads me towards my ego. That begins my journey into supporting my egotistical thinking. Then, all I want to do is talk about me, and I am "the expert." Sometimes, I get lost in that maze. My desires have me chasing along an endless journey of needs and desires. Following this path, I fall into a bottomless pit.

To recover, I uncover the spiritual feelings, or innate health. This feeling is pure because good feelings are always coming from the source of *who I am*. I become unattached, thus I do not need any result to feel good.

This sounds metaphysical, and it is! I do not need anything in order to feel good because I have everything I need right now. I am never broken. I am always healthy. The only strategy I need in order to feel good is to let these feelings happen without judgement, analysis or personal opinion. So, feelings are the answer to everything. Feelings are energy balls, and I want you to love your feelings—yes, I mean, all of them!

**If you want to change anything in your life, plant positive feelings and they will grow, spread and create a beautiful garden.**

**I guarantee it.**

It is the same with addiction. Yes, you probably will have to do some hard work because a life or a garden always requires this. The answer lies in planting positive feelings wherever you walk. Addiction is heavy; it is your negative and fearful feelings about you!

*Plant positive feelings*—watch as your life transforms into a garden of love and healing. *Follow positive feelings*—watch as you uncover the missing link to your happiness and contentment. As the positive feelings build and express, these feelings will release all the common sense you need in order to answer your own questions about life.

There, you will find the answer you seek. I know it does not seem like much, yet it is the truth.


**And then you will step into another world**

**Your world of beautiful feelings!**

# Chapter 29

## Classroom Activity—Why Did I Get Addicted?

In one of the addiction recovery classes I taught, a client lamented: "I cannot understand why I got addicted. I had a great job, had lots of friends, a great family and wife, and my life was very good. It is true that I was doing some cocaine, but it was manageable until it wasn't. Why did I get addicted?"

Different members of the class gave their opinions, with the most relevant stating that he had lost his gratitude. I agreed. Also, I commented that we are always chasing a better feeling, especially when our mood goes down or we feel stressed-out in the moment. Sooner or later, the negative feeling is associated with the need for relief and, in this case, it was the relief provided by cocaine.

While this made sense to him and gave him a glimpse of what he was looking for, it really only halfway answered his question. As the class progressed, another client asked for more teachings in the 3 Principles. When the subject of THOUGHT came up, I specifically aimed my talk to the first client in this story. I suggested that without THOUGHT and CONSCIOUSNESS, he could not see the only window in the room. It required THOUGHT to point at the window, and he needed CONSCIOUSNESS via the five senses to bring it into form. All of a sudden, he gasped, for he had seen how *formlessness creates form*—or, to put it another way—how he creates form via THOUGHT and CONSCIOUSNESS. It was not my words that inspired him; it was the spiritual feeling he experienced in the moment that allowed him to see this. He had stepped into a meditative state of mind, thus experiencing his own insight.

He said to the class, "For four and a half years, I have been wondering why I became an addict, and now I have the answer . . . I saw how THOUGHT allowed me to see the window. If I create form via my thoughts, it is not that far a step to seeing how addiction is created." His face lit up like a glowing sun. He was free in the moment. He had experienced the Principles in action creating the perfect or not-so-perfect psychological reality, depending on his level of CONSCIOUSNESS at that moment in time.

In another recovery class, one of the most unusual clients enjoyed writing down a multitude of phrases on the whiteboard. Then I would teach from these phrases by making reference to the 3 Principles. One day, he wrote "seed of transformation." I was enthralled by that phrase, as I had never really thought about it before. I keyed in on the word *seed* and was reminded of one of my favorite Sydney Banks quotes:

"Purity of Thought are the rungs of the ladder to success."

In this book, *Second Chance*, a main character is asked what his definition of success is, and he answers, "Happiness and contentment." Then, the questioner asks, "What else?" and he replies, "Nothing else." There is only one conclusion. Purity of thought is the *seed* of transformation.

In the addiction field, we are always talking about transformation, and truly this is the fruit of our labors, but the key is the "seed." Without seeds, there are no flowers and no beginnings of transformation. Sometimes seeds take a little while to sprout and grow, but when they do, they are often a powerful surprise and extremely beautiful.

The world needs to arrive at an understanding of what are the *seeds* of addiction, and the *seeds* of transformation.

It is the same understanding.

That understanding will provide the answer to all suffering from addiction, and the delivery of highly evolved recovery programs.

# Chapter 30

# The Power of THOUGHT

I realize that this book conveys many mindsets about THOUGHT. Yet, the help we are looking for in addiction is often gained via an insight or revelation regarding THOUGHT. This book also implies that the solution is seen via a deeper understanding of the Principles of MIND or CONSCIOUSNESS. The 3 Principles are interchangeable and integrated— they are One.

"Are you saying that there is only one principle and

the other two are just there to explain its workings?

"Exactly." Andy replied."

The way I see it, the cure for addiction is simple, although seen from the intellect, it appears quite complicated. God has given us the *free will to think* whatever we want (remember, I am not talking about willpower or positive thinking here).

Let's examine how this works by comparing two potential addiction scenarios:

1. We cannot stop thinking about how we failed, or disappointed ourselves a few days earlier. "How could I be so stupid? How

much better would I feel if I had not done it again? I know I can stop, but I never do! Why do these same thoughts keep coming up? Will they ever go away?" The list is endless. Our thinking spurs on heavy and depressing feelings. It is true that the addiction urge can create a physical, mental and emotional desire to fulfill itself. It is also true that the ego mind loves to feed this urge with an undeniable desire for fulfillment. These thoughts quickly overpower an unknowing or innocent mind, and once again the addicted human can fall victim. The person who is addicted feels powerless. Worse, they love the sensation of chasing this feeling, and then fulfilling it. This re-enforces the pattern of hopelessness and enables caving in to cravings.

2. Then, the thought appears in our consciousness, once again. We experience an *insight* regarding the power of THOUGHT. We do not act on the negative urge this time, thus changing our mind regarding the thought, because we no longer believe in it. The result is instantaneous. We take our consciousness in another direction, and the reality we experience is totally different. This is the psychological purity of the 3 Principles. When we see beyond our little thought system, we bounce back into the spiritual world of gratitude and wonderment. And we forgive ourselves for performing as we did in scenario 1.

This is about how complicated or simple it is. Either we live in a spiritual state of mind, or we don't. When we are addicted, we lose contact with where the power of THOUGHT lies. I am suggesting that it lies within for all us, without exception. When we use this power wisely, everything flows in harmony. We call this love and understanding.

*Lack* of love and understanding sees life differently. Since I have seen that addiction is a negative or fearful thought that we have more or less bought into, it must create an image in our heads (via CONSCIOUSNESS). *This is the law.* This image is what we are fulfilling. This image has created a virtual reality that appears real; in other words, the urge. It needs fulfillment, and it feels temporarily wonderful to satisfy this virtual reality.

Once again, the illusion has provided a falseness or fake-ness that is *not* what we want or need to live a fulfilled life. But there is a silver lining. We see the truth from, of all places, within the ashes of the falseness. We are creating our world of perception via the 3 Principles, and the 3 Principles are the perfect teacher. The teaching—once we see that we are creating our images in our personal mind, we do not have to continue to do it. We have experienced the understanding that this is destructive. The fact is, we love ourselves; it is not wise to continue to hurt or injure ourselves. Misunderstanding this has a devastating effect on our self-esteem, and it creates thoughts of fear and insecurity about us. This is the negative or scared thought that is alluded to in the paragraph above. If you can see the connection between THOUGHT and the image you have created in your own mind, you have uncovered the answer to addiction recovery.

*How do we know which is a spiritual thought and which is an ego thought?* Whether there is a good feeling or bad feelings is the answer.

(I can only express this in a way in that makes sense in terms of what I have experienced.)

If I internally feel the energy or flow of a thought, I calmly navigate toward where MIND is directing me. Energy, rather than the contents of the thought, is the focal point. Our menial repetitive thoughts may nag us from time to time, but they consistently lose power as we use THOUGHT wisely. Vice versa, repetitive thoughts consistently gain power as we use THOUGHT unwisely. But even when we use this power unwisely, we have a second chance every second of our lives, The moment we experience truth, past patterns are broken, and we live life in the Now.

For example, many people have experienced contentment when on vacation. They have forgotten their past problems and just walk into another reality that they love. This reality is like catching a giant wave when we are surfing. It carries us into the "pipe" and out the other side.

Please understand this simple fact. We cannot create doubt or confusion unless we are in a doubtful or confused state of mind. We are living in what we are expressing. If I am self-doubting, then, that is what I must express *until* I see the illusion of the insecurity. Then, I will be safe and express security. Trust in this feeling is the answer that ends the addiction cycle.

**Please use these three spiritual tools wisely,**

**This allows you to escape from many of the pressures, stresses and bad habits of life.**

# Chapter 31

## A Different Way To Talk About the Power of THOUGHT

The *first half of the addiction puzzle* is understanding that "Life is spiritual!" In other words, one must experience an insight or spiritual awakening in order to be free of addiction or any other problems. This is accomplished when the human being walks into the world of silence (no thought), or Oneness.

The *second half of the addiction puzzle* is understanding "the role of THOUGHT"; in other words, an understanding that THOUGHT originates from within and creates in its entirety the world we see and feel. Spiritual or Divine THOUGHT is neutral. What we choose to put into THOUGHT creates our psychological reality. We are the creator of our own perceptions, concepts, beliefs . . . and urges. When one experiences the source, the lucky person also sees the origin of their thoughts, and, ultimately, of their thought patterns. It comes from *inside you.*

Dr. Mark Howard (see Chapter 33) views the Addiction-Recovery-Cycle Model as follows:

1. If we are thinking differently (unwisely) to get relief from stress, we do it in an addictive way.

2. Our suffering and painful feelings are just "habits of thought."

3. Once we catch onto the "nature of THOUGHT" and how any feeling we are having is coming to us by using THOUGHT, we then have insights—this is the healing from addiction!

What this author sees is when we are in a lower level of consciousness, we falsely see that all negative expressions of life come from outside circumstances or past experiences—stubborn parents, lack of money, lack of education, gender, skin color, continual use of opiates or alcohol, and on and on and on it goes.

When we experience a rise in our level of consciousness, we see a whole new world, one in which we are "the thinker," which points to the fact that our state of mind is a key factor to what we are experiencing. If THOUGHT creates feeling, then all one's feelings are a creation of that particular thinker. That is why we have to find the answer to addiction within our own consciousness.

It is important to understand that we cannot mentally change our negative thoughts to positive. Yet when we experience an insight, common sense prevails, and we do not buy into the seriousness of little harmful thoughts; and, more important, we experience the freedom of letting go of serious or speedy thoughts because overthinking is replaced automatically with peace and tranquility—we have once again arrived home! This is why it is a spiritual-psychological answer.

Through arriving home and possessing an understanding of the role of THOUGHT, we are now free from the past memories and experiences that seemed to control us when we were in a lower level of consciousness. When a former urge shows up, it will immediately use all the tricks of the ego to persuade us that it is in control. From the lower level of consciousness, the ego (the urge) is the winner. In a higher level of consciousness, it is the loser.

*Why, you might ask?*

We see that we are experiencing many thoughts in a day, many of which are best to be disregarded, and that this urge is another one to be ignored. One key to understanding the role of THOUGHT is that we do not have to act on all our thoughts! Sydney Banks expressed this in many of his talks.

For example, say a mother is in an extremely bad mood, everything in her body hurts, and she feels that life is trampling on her as she has bills to pay and not enough money. Her husband seems to have lost all interest in her, and as she looks in the mirror, she feels she is getting so old. All of a sudden, her young daughter comes up to her crying because of a bloody nose. Immediately, the mother's nurturing feeling and compassion pours out of her (and all her negative thoughts about her situation vanish), and she takes care of the daughter.

After the daughter goes back to playing, if the mother slips back to the old bad feeling via her thoughts, she will reignite the old feelings detailed above. If she has jumped into a lighter feeling, she will go on with her life, forgetting about all those problems that gave her a feeling of negativity or being a victim of life. She will be following positive feelings that are sustaining. Hooray!

Here is another story that emphasizes the power of THOUGHT. A daughter got into a serious car accident in which her mother was seriously injured. She phoned an ambulance, which arrived shortly. She rode in the ambulance supporting her injured and suffering mother, and she helped her into the emergency room where the mother was immediately operated on.

Eventually, the doctor came out and said the operation went very well and that her mom was going to be fine. The daughter was so relieved. Then the doctor said in a worried tone, "But what about your arm?" She looked at her arm and suddenly realized it was broken and useless. She cried out in excruciating pain. It hurt so badly, yet when her mind was totally fixated on her mom, she did not even notice the broken arm or the pain. That is the power of THOUGHT.

THOUGHT is the most powerful element in our existence, yet our understanding of the role of THOUGHT is so small. This lack of understanding has caused much of the breakdown in society's understanding of how to heal homelessness, mental illness and addiction.

The joke is there is no one wiser than you. All we have to do is learn to listen to our True Self. Sydney Banks had a saying, "A dog that barks up the wrong tree is not much of a hunter." The sad fact is that most humans are followers and have not learned to be very good hunters of truth.

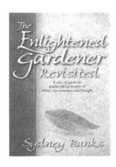

"I'm simply saying it is immaterial why we are creating

our feelings of security or insecurity.

They all derive from our personal usage of this universal gift called *Thought.*"

\* \* \*

"If you have the thought that you are insecure, how do you think you would feel?"

"I imagine I'd feel insecure," I answered.

"Now, that is simplicity in motion, is it not?"

# Chapter 32

## Do We Have Free Will and a Free Mind?

Why would a person who has not had a drink for 30 years consider himself an alcoholic? This person I am thinking of is one of the most content and reasonable humans I have ever met, and yet he sees life from an alcoholic perspective. He has found a level of peace with this concept, and anything outside of this perception confuses and perplexes him.

Let's have a discussion about this.

The way I see it, as long as I agree with what I am thinking in my head, it appears real to me. This is fine when the thoughts are amicable to my general good feelings towards life. When my thoughts seem to run out of control, I feel like a victim.

Accordingly, this is **Question #1** out there in the world of addiction: How can I control my thoughts so that I am not victimized by them? Put another way, how can I gain control of my life?

**Question #2** is a subset of the above question: How can I protect myself or avoid the negative influences of the outside world, circumstances and other people?

First, it is impossible to control our thoughts, so stop trying. Second, those thoughts that are pouring through are mostly irrelevant and not to be taken seriously. I have heard that the average person has nearly 60,000 thoughts each day, many of them repetitive.

- *Can you control your thoughts?*
  "Although we can't 'control' thoughts, we can choose a direction we want our thoughts to flow. Here's where free will or choice comes in."   Elsie Spittle's blog, "Do We Have Choice and Free Will?" (July 23, 2018) www.3phd.net

To add fuel to this discussion, here is a paraphrasing from a tape of Sydney Banks in the late 1970s:

> The game of life is played with a free will and a free mind, and it all stems from CONSCIOUSNESS. God (MIND) is the energy of everything, and psychologically, to explain the game of life, we all have a free will and free mind. Nobody can take it away from us. But there is a *little trick* because our free will and free mind keeps us a prisoner because we have chosen to use our free will instead of submitting to the will of God (MIND). As an actual fact, the will of God (MIND) is the only will that exists. Our own free will and free mind is there because that is how we play our game of life.

* * *

I feel it is best to never underestimate the power of personal thought and how it creates our personal perspective in life. Personal thought is often illusory and irrelevant, while spiritual THOUGHT is neutral, formless and creative. Sometimes I see THOUGHT as the key factor to life, other times I see CONSCIOUSNESS as the key factor. These two Principles are fuelled by the third Principle—the power of MIND. These are not merely three components working together; they intermingle until they arrive at the same point. This point is the Greater Intelligence of Everything or universality of truth.

One time, I experienced that there is no MIND, it is just THOUGHT. I recognize that this may be confusing to the reader, especially since I cannot understand it intellectually myself. I have been expressing MIND as the energy of everything, but even that is THOUGHT. Like I said, sometimes it just *is*. That is a little how I understand "free will."

As a human being, feeling separate from the whole creates a feeling of fear and insecurity. This is the problem in addiction.

---

## HARRY'S BASIC RULE OF THUMB

### *All problems in life are caused by OVERTHINKING.*

---

This means that addiction, temper, violence, rape, mental illness, overeating, boredom, impatience, worry, fear and insecurity—all are caused by overthinking.

*Calm down and relax. Just be yourself.* Of course, many will say this is easier said than done. But, as ordinary human beings, we have this natural reset button. This reset button explains why humans are so resilient. Another term for resiliency is "innate mental health." We are perfectly designed. We are never broken, we never need fixing. Only our own concepts, images and beliefs of life stop us from seeing and experiencing this truth.

To support this idea, I'll share a bit about my dear friend Leo, who lived his life via a powerful insight—that the key to life is in *equilibrium*. He came to see that anything in excess would be destructive to the human condition. If he ate too much one day, he did not eat much the next day. If he did not exercise one day, the next day he made sure he did. It was the same with his thinking. Anything in excess was unhealthy, so he lived as a slim, wise and optimistic man until 100 years old. Equilibrium was his mantra and his way of life. Buddha said it a different way; he talked about inner balance, which means the same thing. Even though Leo had never studied Buddhism, he lived his life like a Buddhist. He simply applied his common sense to his way of living, and coincidentally, Buddha happened to agree with him.

"The trick is you have to go beyond personal truth

to a greater **Spiritual Truth**

that lies deep within your own psyche."

**Where Sydney Banks is pointing to in the above quote is where you will see a clear definition of "free will."**

# Chapter 33

# Do Other Leading Professionals See the 3 Principles as the Ultimate Answer to Addiction?

The essence of this chapter is the million-dollar question: Are the Principles the ultimate answer to all suffering? If so, then they will obviously transform the world of addiction recovery over time. If they are not, then they will just become another mousetrap that is either better than or not as good as the 12-Step approach.

Here is the fact: *They will transform addiction recovery.* When this will happen, I don't know, but it is inevitable.

\* \* \*

***Dr. William Pettit Jr.,*** MD, is a board-certified psychiatrist and co-owner of 3 Principles Intervention LLC. He has spent the majority of his career awakening mental health and the sharing of the understanding that there is just one cause—and one cure—for mental illness. Dr. Pettit is a recognized educator in the 3 Principles intervention, and he has presented at many national and international conferences, as well as consulted to numerous clients both nationally and internationally.

> In 1983, I had been in the field of psychiatry for nearly 10 years. I was discouraged professionally in that all I really had to help patients was medication. Personally, I had been struggling with intermittent depression and had sought help from six different psychiatrists. I met Dr. George Pransky early in 1983, and shortly thereafter, with his encouragement, I attended a weekend program presented by Sydney Banks. Within the first 20 minutes, I realized that Mr. Banks knew much more about mental well-being than I did.

I soon came to see that everyone had perfect mental well-being and that no one is ever broken. That certainty, via incremental insights into the three universal Principles, allowed me to find my own mental health and to speak directly to that health in others.

Once people feel that we care, they are interested in hearing what we know. Since 1983, I have been able to help people of all major diagnostic categories including *life-threatening addiction* to come home to a state of mental well-being and peace. Being a psychiatrist has become joyful and filled with wonder at the human spirit. Love and understanding are the curative agents.

*  *  *

*Joseph Bailey*, M.A., L.P., is a licensed clinical psychologist and best-selling author of six books, including *The Serenity Principle*. As of the publication of this book, his next volume will be *The Transformation Principle*. He has spoken around the world to various treatment centres and professional conferences on a 3 Principles-based approach to addiction and mental health issues, including Gulf Breeze Recovery Center in Florida and Farnum Center in New Hampshire.

This approach has been utilized for the past 35 years in a variety of inpatient and outpatient settings with promising and often dramatic results. Instead of focusing on the addiction itself as the problem, the 3 Principles understanding of addiction treatment focuses on bringing out the innate health or serenity of the client by educating him or her in the scientific and logical principles that underlie the human experience. When innate health is awakened in clients, their incentive to relapse, transfer addictions, or still be unhappy but sober, often changes dramatically. Clients report a lack of desire to look "outside" for solutions and feelings that are realized naturally through deepening understanding of how the mind actually creates our life experience. .

* * *

***Dr. Amy Johnson***, PhD, is a psychologist, coach, author, and speaker who shares a 3 Principles approach that helps people find true, lasting freedom from unwanted habits via insight rather than willpower. She is author of several books including *The Little Book of Big Change: The No-Willpower Approach to Breaking Any Habit* (2016); and in 2017, she opened The Little School of Big Change. She has been a regularly featured expert on *The Steve Harvey Show* and Oprah.com, as well as in *The Wall Street Journal* and *Self* magazine.

As Harry says, when we move from trying to fix the "problem" of addiction, to speaking to the spirit in those who are suffering, consciousness rises and incredible transformation often takes place. I have unequivocally seen this to be true with my own clients, and I know it is true for others who share these Principles that Harry points toward. *The Evolution of Addiction* points to what can be a complete paradigm shift in treating addiction, as well as in how we view mental health.

People I'm working with for the first time often wonder why they didn't experience deep, lasting change in the past despite the fact that they did "all the right things" . . . They talked to the right people about their problems. They paid the money and put in the time and effort. In the case of anxiety, rumination, insecurity, or fear, they were mindful. They meditated or observed or whatever it is that people doing mindfulness do. In the case of unwanted behaviors, habits, and addictions, they abstained. They added new things to their lives to take the place of bad habits. They busied themselves and steered clear of old triggers.

*Why didn't their change stick?* They want to know.

* * *

**Dr. Mark Howard**, PhD, Psychologist. Since 1982, Dr. Mark Howard has trained a large number of 3 Principles practitioners in North America, United Kingdom, and Europe. He also has brought his expertise in teaching the principles to mental health practitioners at a major medical center where he mentored eight psychologists for two years to hundreds of health practitioners in many diverse fields at Santa Clara County for 18 years. He has developed the Addiction Recovery Cycle Model based on the 3 Principles.

> I believe the understanding of the Principles is an opportunity for you to access the wisdom and intelligence within you to overcome your life struggles. With over 30 years in practice, I have helped people who were suffering from anxiety, depression. low self-esteem, behaviors like compulsive shopping, *substance abuse*, academic failure and spiritual doubts. As your understanding of the 3 Principles deepens, you will demonstrate more of the human attributes that help you in life, whether dealing with your job, your relationships or yourself. .

* * *

As you have seen, in the world in which I live, the 3 Principles as uncovered by Sydney Banks are not a better mousetrap; they are spiritual principles that create our psychological reality in totality—in other words, all the good or bad stuff that humans experience.

The creation of addiction is the same power as the creation of love and understanding. This is revolutionary. What we do with the Principles is key and fundamental to how we experience life. We use the Principles wisely, or unwisely. It's as simple and impersonal as that.

*REFERENCE: Appearances by the above-mentioned professionals on the* **Addiction, Alcoholism & The 3 Principles** *YouTube series*

| | |
|---|---|
| https://youtu.be/fogC633AdOQ | Dr. Bill Pettit on "Nothing Broken, Nothing Lacking" |
| https://youtu.be/MQdVj_8c_vg | Dr. Bill Pettit on "Psychological Innocence" |
| https://youtu.be/hUzSsx1op7I | Dr. Amy Johnson on "Big Change" |
| https://youtu.be/rd687-2aCA0 | Dr. Joseph Bailey on "The Evolution of Recovery" |
| https://youtu.be/XeuMEel0UK8 | Dr. Mark Howard on "The Addiction Model Cycle" |

# Chapter 34

# My Vision for the World of Addiction

In my opinion, Sydney Banks's dream was for everyone to see that truth lies within. He states in the Introduction of his book *The Missing Link*, "If these writings bring a second chance of life to just one human being, my work has not been in vain." He uncovered these three sacred Principles as a guiding light to the cure of all suffering, and as a pointer to happiness and contentment.

Sydney Banks's materials—books, videos and audios—are invaluable. His story, as a living example of how a simple and ordinary man, with many normal problems, had one profound spiritual insight that totally changed not only his life but thousands of lives, and potentially millions, is a story of inspiration. My own life is a living testimony to this.

This book is an attempt to lay out a roadmap for those interested in or affected by the world of addiction. Individual 3P professionals, who have learned from Sydney Banks and other leading 3P teachers, will carve their own paths of contribution in the area of addiction. Some will write books, develop courses and work in collaboration with others in state-of-the-art programs and conferences. New practitioners will arrive with a need for some specific support, and, hopefully, this will be provided. There will be growth that is organic and free flowing. I would love to see those who work with addictions create a program based on the 3 Principles and become successful to where the teaching is accepted by the addicted and alcoholic world as an ultimate solution—to be an evolution to take humankind onto a wiser path for solving the opiate and addiction crisis that this world finds itself in.

It is said that more are dying from pharmaceutical drugs than street drugs. Clients with addiction, rich and poor, and from all walks of life and cultures, want to examine the truth within—this truth that is the

**ultimate answer** to all their suffering. Every human being wants and needs this.

Humanity evolves as it awakens. Please walk into the world of happiness and contentment with me. There, we will find the sunken treasure that lies at the deepest part of "who you are." There, we will uncover the greatest gift in the universe—MIND (God, Spirit) is always providing everything we need and more, not just to you but to everyone, all the time and in all circumstances. It is called "the perfect design" or the "perfection of our lives." You will feel safe and secure in this, and, by the way, I would love to see a smile on your face right now. You deserve it!

### *THIS IS THE END OF BOOK ONE.*

Made in the USA
Columbia, SC
06 February 2019